Franklin GRE Word List

3861 GRE Words For
High GRE Verbal Score

from
Franklin GRE Vocab Builder
Audio Program

**Includes Free Bonus Book at
the End of This Book**
GRE 1851 Most
Difficult Words

By Franklin Vocab System

For FREE CD Download
(Please see the last page of this book)

Support Email: sale@FranklinVocab.com

Table of Contents

Why is GRE Vocab So Hard?

It may surprise you that GRE tends to test you for meanings that are not the most common meanings of words.

For example, here are some words and the meanings you need to know (taken from the course). I have also added the meaning that will not lead to correct answer:

milk = extract
USE = the directors milked the company of several million dollars
(not the milk you drink)

stole = long scarf
USE = a mink stole
(not a form of steal)

riddle = to make many holes in, permeate
USE = the anti-aircraft guns riddled the plane's wings with bullets
(not a puzzle)

root = to dig
USE = she rooted through the papers on her desk
(not root of a tree)

kite = bad check
USE = *
(not a kite that people fly)

rifle = search through and steal
USE = the safe had been rifled and the diamonds were gone
(not the rifle used for firing bullets)

ejaculate = exclaim
USE = You've got my umbrella! he ejaculated
(not sex related ejaculation)

This Book Gives You Only One or Two Important Meanings and "Short Memorable Sentence Fragments", Making it Easier to Remember

(not too many meanings or long sentences)

You don't get 3 or 5 or 10 meanings and sentences that are impossible to remember (a dictionary is better if you want to do PhD on some aspects of words). I give you short and memorable sentence fragments, so you can remember faster and better. Here are some examples (please notice how easily memorable the sentence fragments are):

euphoria = elation, feeling of well-being or happiness

USE = in a state of euphoria

evade = to avoid

USE = don't evade taxes

excerpt = selection from a book, extract

USE = excerpt of a new book

illicit = unlawful, illegal

USE = illicit liquor

immense = huge

USE = at immense cost

de facto = actual

USE = de facto standard (Not full sentence)

draconian = harsh

USE = draconian laws

prodigy = a person with extraordinary ability or talent

USE = a child prodigy

eke = to add to, supplement

USE = to eke out a living

Herculean = powerful, large

USE = a Herculean task

pyrrhic = a battle won with unacceptable losses

USE = a pyrrhic victory

How is this Word List Organized

This book contains the words, meanings, and sentence fragments.

These same words and information are also recorded on 19 CDs available to you as download (The last page of this book has the details on how to get download link).

The words are given in bold (example, the words **belabor** and **buttress** below). The meaning is given after the equal sign (=) following a word.

The words are not necessarily in alphabetical order.

We have used the US spellings. The British spelling of a word, when different from the US spelling, is given in bracket after BRITISH as shown for the word **belabor** below.

USE gives a sentence fragment carefully chosen for memory. When no sentence fragment is given, a * is shown as in the word **buttress** below.

> **belabor** (BRITISH = belabour) = to assail verbally, to insist repeatedly or harp on
> USE = belabor a point
>
> **buttress** = support
> USE = *

CD 1

amphitheater (BRITISH = amphitheatre) = oval-shaped theater
USE = we watched the play at the amphitheater

anathema = curse, ban
USE = For older employees, the new system is an anathema

annul = cancel, nullify
USE = annul a law

anodyne = pain soothing
USE = This is daytime TV at its most anodyne

anoint = consecrate, to apply oil, especially as a sacred rite
USE = to anoint as a successor

anonymity = state of being anonymous, having no name
USE = they were guaranteed anonymity

antediluvian = ancient, obsolete, pre historic
USE = hopelessly antediluvian ideas

antithesis = direct opposite
USE = She is slim and shy - the very antithesis of her sister

apathetic = unconcerned, indifferent
USE = Young people today are so apathetic about politics

aphasia = inability to speak or use words
USE = suffer from aphasia

aphorism = maxim, old saying
USE = *

aplomb = poise, confidence
USE = with her usual aplomb

apocryphal = a doubtful authenticity, not genuine, fictional
USE = an apocryphal story

apostate = one who abandons one's faith
USE = because he switched parties, his former friends shunned him as an apostate

apotheosis = Deification, glorification
USE = the apotheosis of a Roman emperor

approbation = praise, official approval
USE = The council has finally indicated its approbation of the plans

archaic = Antiquated, from an earlier time
USE = an archaic law

archipelago = group of islands
USE = the Hawaiian archipelago

ardor (BRITISH = ardour) = great emotion or passion
USE = His ardor for her cooled after only a few weeks

arraign = indict, to call to court to answer a charge
USE = He was arraigned on charges of aiding and abetting terrorists

arrogate = seize without right, to demand or claim arrogantly
USE = They arrogate to themselves the power to punish people

ascendancy = powerful state
USE = They are in the danger of losing their political ascendancy

ascribe = to attribute
USE = To what do you ascribe your phenomenal success?

ashen = resembling ashes, or deathly pale
USE = She was thin and her face was ashen

asinine = stupid
USE = an asinine comment

askance = to view with suspicion, scornfully
USE = They looked askance at our scruffy clothes

askew = crooked, tilted
USE = My hat was askew so I adjusted it in the mirror

aspersion = slander, false rumor, damaging report
USE = cast aspersions on

assail = attack
USE = He was assailed with insults and abuse

assent = to express agreement
USE = She nodded her assent to the proposal.

assiduous = hard-working, diligent, persistent
USE = assiduous research

assuage = lessen (pain), to make less severe, ease
USE = The government has tried to assuage the public's fears

astringent = causing contraction, severe, harsh
USE = astringent criticism

asunder = apart, into different parts
USE = torn asunder

atone = make amends for a wrong
USE = a wish to atone for his actions in the past

august = noble, dignified, awe-inspiring, venerable
USE = the society's august patron, the former maharaja of Jaipur

avow = declare
USE = He avowed that he regretted what he had done

awry = crooked, askew, amiss
USE = The strike has sent the plans for investment seriously awry

axiom = self-evident truth, premise, postulate
USE = It is a widely held axiom that

bacchanal = orgy, drunkenly festive
USE = Emperor Nero attended the bacchanalian orgy.

baleful = hostile, malignant, harmful with evil intentions
USE = his baleful influence

balk = hesitate, refuse, shirk, prevent
USE = to balk at the prospect of

banal = trite, overly common
USE = banal pop songs

bane = poison, nuisance, something causing ruin
USE = Keeping noise levels low is the bane of airport administration

bastion = fort, fortification, stronghold
USE = the last bastions of upper-class privilege

beguile = deceive, seduce, mislead
USE = He was completely beguiled by her beauty.

behemoth = monster, huge creature
USE = a grocery chain behemoth

beleaguer = besiege, to harass, plague
USE = the beleaguered doctors working in the refugee camps

berate = to scold harshly
USE = As he left the meeting, he was berated by angry demonstrators

bestial = beast-like, brutal
USE = The soldiers were accused of bestial acts against unarmed civilians

bestow = to give as a gift, grant
USE = The Chancellorship of the University was bestowed upon her in 2003

bevy = group
USE = a bevy of parrots

bicker = quarrel, to have a petty argument
USE = Will you two stop bickering!

bilious = ill-tempered
USE = a bilious old man

bilk = swindle, cheat, defraud
USE = The con man specialized in bilking insurance companies

blandish = to coax with flattering, grovel
USE = she did not respond to his blandishments

blight = decay, afflict, destroy
USE = cast a blight on

blithe = Joyful, cheerful, or without appropriate thought
USE = She shows a blithe disregard for danger

bombast = pompous speech
USE = a bombastic statement

bourgeois = middle class
USE = It's a bit bourgeois, isn't it, joining a golf club

broach = bring up a topic of conversation
USE = I don't know how to broach the subject with him

brusque = curt, rough and abrupt in manner
USE = His secretary was rather brusque with me

bulwark = fortification
USE = My savings were to be a bulwark against unemployment

burgeon = sprout or flourish
USE = Love burgeoned between them

burly = husky, brawny
USE = a burly policeman

cabal = plot, a secret group seeking to overturn something
USE = He was assassinated by a cabal of aides within his own regime

cadaver = corpse, dead body
USE = in some countries, it is illegal to dissect cadavers

cajole = encourage, coax, flatter
USE = He really knows how to cajole people into doing what he wants

calumny = Slander, false and malicious accusation
USE = He was subjected to the most vicious calumny

canard = hoax, a lie
USE = it is difficult to protect oneself from such a base canard

candor (BRITISH = candour) = frankness, honesty of expression
USE = "We really don't know what to do about it, " she said with surprising candor

canvass = survey, examine thoroughly
USE = to canvass local opinion

capricious = fickle, impulsive, whimsical, without much thought
USE = a capricious child

careen = swerve, to lean on one side
USE = when the brakes failed, the car went careening down the hill

castigate = criticize, punish, chastise
USE = Health inspectors castigated the kitchen staff for poor standards of cleanliness

cataclysm = catastrophe, disaster
USE = they feared a nuclear cataclysm

cathartic = purgative, purifying, cleansing
USE = a cathartic experience

catholic = universal, worldly
USE = As a young person he had more catholic tastes than he does now

caucus = a small group within an organization or a meeting of such a group
USE = the party held a caucus to elect a leader

cavil = quibble, raise trivial objections
USE = The one cavil I have about the book is that it is written as a diary

cede = transfer ownership, to surrender possession of something
USE = Hong Kong was ceded to Britain after the Opium War

censorious = condemning speech, severely critical
USE = censorious people delight in casting blame

chagrin = shame, embarrassment, humiliation
USE = My children have never shown an interest in music, much to my chagrin

chalice = goblet, cup
USE = they drank from a chalice

chary = cautious, watchful, extremely shy
USE = I'm a bit chary of using a travel agency that doesn't have official registration

cherubic = sweet, innocent
USE = the child with a cherubic face

chicanery = trickery, fraud, deception
USE = political chicanery and corruption

chide = scold, express disapproval
USE = She chided him for his bad manners

chimerical = imaginary, impossible
USE = a chimerical solution would not solve the problem

choleric = easily angered, short-tempered
USE = his angry face indicated a choleric nature

circumlocution = roundabout expression
USE = Politicians are experts in circumlocution

circumspect = cautious, wary
USE = Officials were circumspect about what the talks had achieved

circumvent = evade, avoid, to go around
USE = Ships were registered abroad to circumvent employment regulations

citadel = fortress or stronghold
USE = The town has a 14th century citadel overlooking the river

clamor (BRITISH = clamour) = noisy outcry
USE = Fans were clamoring for their autographs

cleave = to split or separate, to stick, adhere
USE = The ancient ivy cleaved to the ruined castle walls

clemency = forgiveness, merciful leniency
USE = The jury passed a verdict of guilty, with an appeal to the judge for clemency

cloister = refuge, to confine, seclude
USE = the nuns lived in a cloister

coalesce = combine, to grow together
USE = the brooks coalesce into a large river

coddle = to pamper, baby, treat indulgently
USE = The steel industry is coddled by trade protection and massive subsidies

cogent = well-put, convincing, logically forceful
USE = cogent reply

cognate = from the same source, related
USE = The Italian word 'mangiare' is cognate with the French 'manger', both of which mean 'to eat'

cognomen = family name, any name, nickname
USE = he asked the court to change his cognomen to a more American-sounding name

colloquy = conference
USE = I enjoy our colloquies, but sometimes wish for a more formal approach

collusion = conspiracy, collaboration, complicity
USE = they worked in collusion with the terrorist network

commodious = spacious
USE = a commodious house

complicity = guilt by association, knowing partnership in wrong doing
USE = She is suspected of complicity in the fraud

compunction = remorse, regret
USE = I wouldn't have any compunction about telling him to leave

concur = To agree
USE = The new report concurs with previous findings

conflagration = large fire, big, destructive fire
USE = a full-blown regional conflagration

confluence = flowing together, meeting of two streams, meeting place
USE = Allahabad is a confluence of three rivers

confound = bewilder, to baffle, perplex
USE = The dancer confounded her critics with a remarkable performance

congeal = solidify, as a liquid freezing, to become thick or solid
USE = The blood had congealed in thick black clots

conjecture = hypothesis, speculation, prediction
USE = a lot of conjecture in the papers

conjure = summon, to evoke a spirit, cast a spell
USE = In an instant, the magician had conjured up a cat from his hat.

consanguinity = related by blood, kinship
USE = the law suit developed into a test of consanguinity of the claimant to the estate

consecrate = make holy, dedicate to a goal, to declare sacred
USE = The new temple was completed and consecrated in 1962

construe = interpret or to explain
USE = Any change in plan would be construed as indecision

continence = self-control, self-restraint
USE = she vowed to lead a life of continence

contrite = apologetic, deeply sorrowful and repentant for a wrong
USE = a contrite apology

contusion = A bruise
USE = she was treated for contusions and abrasions

conundrum = enigma, puzzle or problem with no solution, riddle
USE = Arranging childcare over the school holidays can be quite a conundrum for working parents

convivial = sociable, festive, fond of eating, drinking, and people
USE = a convivial atmosphere

convoke = convene, summon, to call together
USE = convocation ceremony

coquette = woman who flirts
USE = because she did not reply to his proposal for marriage, he called her a coquette

corroborate = to confirm, verify
USE = Recent research seems to corroborate his theory

coterie = small group, group of people with a common interest or purpose
USE = a coterie of writers

countenance = facial expression, to favor, support
USE = He was of noble countenance

cower = showing fear, to cringe in fear
USE = Stop cowering! I'm not going to hit you

crass = crude, unrefined
USE = crass behavior

craven = cowardly
USE = a craven act of terrorism

credence = Belief, acceptance of something as true or real
USE = I'm not prepared to give credence to anonymous complaints

creed = Belief or principle
USE = in any Indian's creed, love for democracy must be emphasized

cringe = cower, to shrink in fear
USE = He cringed at the sight of his dad dancing

culpable = blameworthy, guilty, responsible for wrong
USE = He was held culpable

cupidity = greed
USE = the cupidity of the conquerors

curmudgeon = boor, cranky person
USE = though regarded by many as a curmudgeon, he secretly donated to charity

dally = procrastinate, to act playfully or waste time
USE = He dallied with the idea of starting his own business

debase = to degrade, or lower in quality or stature
USE = Some argue that money has debased cricket

debauch = to corrupt, seduce from virtue or duty
USE = a vicious newspaper can debauch public ideals

debutante = a girl debuting into society
USE = a debutantes' ball

decadence = deterioration, decay (e.g. moral or cultural)
USE = Western decadence

decapitate = kill by beheading
USE = some soldiers were decapitated

deciduous = shedding leaves, short-lived, temporary
USE = the oak is a deciduous tree

decorous = seemly, proper, tasteful, socially correct
USE = His manner, as ever, was decorous

decry = castigate, to belittle, openly condemn
USE = She decried the appalling state of the film industry

deference = courteously yielding to another, respect, honor
USE = He treats her with such deference

defile = pollute, to make unclean or dishonor
USE = The soldiers deliberately defiled all the holy places

deft = skillful, dexterous
USE = deft and quick

defunct = extinct, no longer existing, dead
USE = members of a now defunct communist organization

deleterious = harmful, destructive, detrimental
USE = deleterious effect on the nervous system

deluge = a flood, to submerge, overwhelm
USE = This little stream can become a deluge when it rains heavily

demagogue = An unprincipled politician, leader
USE = he was accused of being a demagogue because he aroused false hopes in people

demean = to degrade, humiliate, humble
USE = The entire family was demeaned by his behavior

demur = take exception, to express doubts or objections
USE = The lawyer requested a break in the court case, but the judge demurred

denigrate = defame, to slur or blacken someone's reputation
USE = You shouldn't denigrate people just because they have different beliefs from you

depravity = immorality, sinfulness
USE = a depraved character

deprecate = belittle, disparage
USE = We deprecate this use of company funds for political purposes

deride = To ridicule, to mock, make fun of
USE = He derided my singing as pathetic

desecrate = profane, to abuse something sacred
USE = It's a crime to desecrate the country's flag

desiccate = dehydrate, to dry completely
USE = people desiccate food in order to preserve it

despondent = depressed, feeling discouraged and dejected
USE = She started to feel despondent about ever finding a job

desultory = without direction in life, at random, rambling, unmethodical
USE = She made a desultory attempt at conversation

diatribe = long denunciation, bitter verbal attack
USE = He launched into a long diatribe against the government's policies

dichotomy = a division into two parts
USE = a dichotomy between what politicians say and what they do

didactic = instructional
USE = a didactic approach to teaching

dilettante = amateur, dabbler
USE = He's a bit of a dilettante as far as wine is concerned

disabuse = correct, to free from a misconception
USE = He thought that all women liked children, but she soon disabused him of that idea

disburse = pay out
USE = The local authorities annually disburse 2 crores of Rupees on arts projects

disconsolate = inconsolable, unable to be consoled, extremely sad
USE = The team were disconsolate after losing what should have been an easy game

discrete = separate, distinct
USE = Many companies have their own discrete identity

discursive = rambling, wandering from topic to topic
USE = a discursive writer

disdain = to regard with scorn and contempt
USE = He regards the political process with disdain

disingenuous = deceptive, sly and crafty
USE = It was disingenuous of her to claim she had no financial interest in the case

disjointed = disconnected, incoherent, being separated
USE = The script was disjointed and hard to follow

disparage = belittle, speak disrespectfully about
USE = The actor's work for charity has recently been disparaged in the press as an attempt to get publicity

disparate = various, dissimilar, different in kind
USE = The two cultures were utterly disparate

disparity = difference, contrast, dissimilarity
USE = the disparity between rich and poor

dispirit = discourage, to dishearten, make dejected
USE = the team had become dispirited at the loss of their star player

dissipate = scatter
USE = The heat gradually dissipates into the atmosphere

distend = swell, inflate, bloat
USE = In the refugee centers we saw many children whose stomachs were distended because of lack of food

distraught = distressed, very worried
USE = The missing child's distraught parents

docile = domesticated, trained, tame
USE = The once docile population has finally risen up against the ruthless regime

dotage = senility, mental decline
USE = in his dotage, the old man bored everyone

dour = sullen and gloomy, stern and severe
USE = The normally dour Mr. Jay was photographed smiling

droll = amusing in a wry
USE = a droll remark

dulcet = melodious, pleasant sounding
USE = the dulcet sounds of birds at the dawn

duplicity = deceit, treachery, dishonesty, double-dealing
USE = They were accused of duplicity in their dealings with both sides

duress = coercion, imprisonment
USE = he signed the confession under duress

ebb = recede, to fade away
USE = He could feel his strength ebbing away

ebullient = exuberant, full of enthusiasm and high spirits
USE = He wasn't his usual ebullient self

eclectic = from various sources
USE = an eclectic taste in literature

edify = instruct morally and spiritually
USE = I watch the television for pleasure rather than edification

efface = To obliterate
USE = The whole country had tried to efface the memory of the old dictatorship

effrontery = insolence
USE = He was silent all through the meal and then had the effrontery to complain that I looked bored

effulgent = brilliant
USE = the effulgent rays of the rising sun lit the sky

elicit = provoke
USE = to elicit a response from someone

elucidate = make clear, clarify
USE = I don't understand. You'll have to elucidate

emaciated = underfed, gaunt
USE = pictures of emaciated children

embroil = involve, cause to fall into disorder
USE = The United Nations was reluctant to get its forces embroiled in civil war

emend = correct
USE = The text is currently being emended

encomium = warm praise
USE = encomiums and panegyrics expressed by speakers

encumber = burden, to hinder, restrict motion
USE = does wearing saree encumber mothers in running after their babies

endemic = Peculiar to some specified country or people
USE = Malaria is endemic in India

enervate = weaken, sap strength from
USE = I find this heat very enervating

engender = generate, to produce
USE = Her latest book has engendered a lot of controversy

enigmatic = puzzling, inexplicable
USE = The Mona Lisa has a famously enigmatic smile

enjoin = urge, order, command
USE = We were all enjoined to be on our best behavior

ennui = boredom, lack of interest and energy
USE = ennui of winter

enthrall (BRITISH = enthral) = mesmerize, to captivate, enchant
USE = The cricket match completely enthralled the crowd

entreat = plead, beg
USE = parents spent time entreating the child to eat vegetable

epicure = gourmet, person with refined taste in food and wine
USE = epicures frequent his restaurant because of exotic food

epigram = saying, short, witty saying or poem
USE = a frequently quoted epigram

epithet = name, appellation, phrase
USE = The singer's 104-kilo frame has earned him the epithet of 'Man Mountain' in the press

equine = pertaining to horses
USE = equine flu

erode = wear away, to diminish
USE = The cliffs are eroding several feet a year, erode confidence in his judgment

errant = wandering, mistaken
USE = an errant husband

eschew = avoid, to abstain from
USE = We won't have discussions with this group unless they eschew violence

espouse = to support or advocate
USE = she espouses vegetarianism

estranged = alienated, separated
USE = the estranged wife sought a divorce

euthanasia = mercy-killing
USE = campaign for the right to euthanasia

evanescent = fleeting, very brief, short-lived
USE = evanescent fame

evince = attest, demonstrate, to show clearly
USE = They have never evinced any readiness or ability to negotiate

CD 2

lineage = ancestry
USE = She's very proud of her ancient royal lineage

listless = lacking spirit or interest
USE = The illness left him listlesshint

livid = enraged, reddened with anger
USE = He was livid when he found out

lofty = high, elevated in position
USE = a lofty ceiling

lucid = clearly understood
USE = a lucid explanation

ludicrous = absurd, laughable
USE = a ludicrous idea

luminous = bright
USE = a luminous object

magnanimous = generous, kindhearted
USE = the manager was magnanimous in victory, and praised the losing team

magnate = a powerful, successful person
USE = a well-known shipping magnate

magnitude = greatness of size
USE = They don't seem to grasp the magnitude of the problem

maladroit = clumsy
USE = She can be a little maladroit in social situations

malleable = moldable, tractable, capable of being shaped
USE = Lead and tin are malleable metals

mandatory = obligatory, necessary
USE = mandatory drugs test

manifest = obvious, evident
USE = illness first manifested itself

mentor = teacher, wise adviser
USE = the child found a new mentor to excel him at cricket

mercenary = calculating, venal
USE = mercenary motives

metamorphosis = a change in form
USE = metamorphosis of caterpillar to butterfly

meticulous = extremely careful, precise
USE = meticulous preparation

militate = work against
USE = The slowness of the judicial system militates against justice for the individual.

millennium = one thousand years
USE = How did you celebrate the Millennium

minuscule = small
USE = two minuscule pieces of toast

misanthrope = hater of mankind
USE = *

misgiving = doubt
USE = misgivings about the new policy

misnomer = wrongly named
USE = It's something of a misnomer

mitigate = lessen the severity
USE = to mitigate the risk

momentous = of great importance
USE = a momentous decision

morose = sullen, gloomy
USE = a morose expression

mundane = ordinary, worldly
USE = Mundane matters

myopic = narrow-minded, near-sighted
USE = the myopic refusal to act now

nadir = lowest point
USE = The defeat was the nadir of her career

nebulous = indistinct, cloudy, vague
USE = a few nebulous ideas

nefarious = evil, vicious
USE = nefarious practices

nicety = euphemism, minute distinction
USE = We don't bother with all the social niceties here

nocturnal = pertaining to night
USE = Most bats are nocturnal.

nomenclature = terms used in a particular science or discipline
USE = nomenclature of organic chemicals

nominal = slight, existing in name only
USE = nominal fees

novice = beginner
USE = I've never driven a car before - I'm a complete novice

noxious = toxic, harmful
USE = a noxious smell

nuance = shade of meaning, subtlety
USE = Linguists explore the nuances of language

nullify = void
USE = the law was nullified

obscure = vague, unclear, dim
USE = His answers were obscure and confusing

obsolete = outdated
USE = Kerosene lamps became obsolete when electric lighting was invented

obviate = make unnecessary
USE = A peaceful solution would obviate the need to send a military force.

officious = forward, obtrusive
USE = an officious little man

ominous = threatening, indicating misfortune
USE = ominous dark clouds

Omnipotent = all-powerful
USE = an omnipotent king

omniscient = all-knowing
USE = the omniscient narrator

opaque = nontransparent
USE = opaque glass

opportune = well-timed
USE = an opportune moment

optimum = best condition
USE = an optimum choice

opulence = wealth
USE = he has only known opulence

oscillate = to move back and forth
USE = My emotions oscillate between desperation and hope

palatial = grand, splendid
USE = he owned a palatial house

panacea = cure-all
USE = Technology is not a panacea for all our problems

panorama = vista, broad view
USE = From the hotel roof you can enjoy a panorama of the whole city

paraphrase = restatement
USE = to paraphrase, what it means is

parity = equality
USE = pay parity

parody = imitation, ridicule
USE = he wrote parodies of other people's works

patronize = condescend, disparage, to buy from
USE = We always patronize Taj Restaurant - the food is so good there

paucity = scarcity
USE = a paucity of information

pedestrian = common, unimaginative
USE = he wrote page after page of pedestrian prose

penury = extreme poverty
USE = the painter lived in penury

perpetual = continuous
USE = in perpetual fear

perturbation = agitation, disturbance
USE = Perturbations in the orbit of the planet Uranus led to the discovery of Neptune

phobia = fear, anxiety
USE = a phobia of worms

pillage = plunder, to loot
USE = Works of art were pillaged from many countries

pinnacle = highest point of development
USE = the pinnacle of her career

pious = devout, holy, extremely religious
USE = a pious follower of the religion

placate = appease, to soothe
USE = Outraged minority groups will not be placated by promises of future improvements

podium = stand, rostrum, platform
USE = she stood on the winner's podium

ponderous = heavy, bulky
USE = a slow and ponderous manner

posterity = future generations
USE = to preserve for posterity

pragmatic = practical
USE = the pragmatic approach to problems

precarious = dangerous, risky
USE = precarious financial position

precipitate = cause, sudden and unexpected
USE = Fear of losing her job precipitated her into action

preclude = To prevent
USE = *

preeminent (BRITISH = pre-eminent) = supreme, distinguished
USE = pre-eminent scientist

premonition = warning
USE = She had a sudden premonition of what the future might bring

presumptuous = assuming, improperly bold
USE = It would be presumptuous of me to comment on this matter

pretext = excuse
USE = He came round to see her on some flimsy pretext

prevaricate = lie
USE = He accused the minister of prevaricating

pristine = pure, unspoiled
USE = pristine beaches

profane = impure, contrary to religion
USE = profane language

prolific = fruitful, productive
USE = prolific writer

propriety = appropriateness
USE = he was careful always to behave with propriety

prostrate = lying flat on the ground
USE = he prostrated himself before the god idol

protocol = code of diplomatic etiquette
USE = royal protocol

provincial = intolerant, insular, limited in scope
USE = provincial governments

proximity = nearness
USE = The best thing about the location of the house is its proximity to the market

proxy = substitute, agent
USE = a proxy vote

pseudonym = alias, pen name
USE = the author used a pseudonym

pundit = learned or politically astute person
USE = a political pundit

punitive = punishing
USE = punitive action

purge = cleanse, remove
USE = Party leaders have undertaken to purge the party of extremists

quack = charlatan, fake
USE = quacks operate eyes and at times cause blindness

quadruped = four foot animal
USE = cow is a quadruped

quarantine = detention, confinement, isolation period
USE = The horse had to spend several months in quarantine when it reached India

rail = rant, harangue, to complain angrily
USE = He railed against the injustices of the system

ramification = consequence
USE = Have you considered all the ramifications of your suggestion

rancid = rotten
USE = rancid oil

ravage = plunder, to destroy
USE = a country ravaged by war

rebuff = reject
USE = She rebuffed all suggestions that she should resign

recapitulate = restate, summarize
USE = finally the speaker recapitulated the main points

rectify = correct
USE = to rectify the situation

redress = restitution
USE = redress the problem

refurbish = remodel
USE = He refurbished the house inside and out

refute = disprove
USE = refute the allegations

reiterate = repeat
USE = reiterate the demands

rejuvenate = make young again
USE = take a vacation to rejuvenate

relinquish = release
USE = She relinquished her hold/grip on the steering wheel

relish = savor, to enjoy greatly
USE = I always relish a challenge

renounce = to give up or reject a right
USE = Gandhi ji renounced the use of violence

residue = remaining part
USE = The white residue in the bucket is a result of minerals in the water

resuscitate = revive
USE = Her heart had stopped, but the doctors successfully resuscitated her

retrospective = looking back to the past
USE = the change in law was retrospective

rhetoric = persuasive use of language
USE = election campaign rhetoric

rift = a split, an opening
USE = a deep rift in the rock

robust = vigorous
USE = a robust economy

saccharine = sugary, overly sweet tone
USE = I don't trust her, with her saccharine smiles

salient = prominent
USE = salient features of a product

sanction = approval
USE = His leave application was sanctioned

satiate = satisfy fully
USE = He drank greedily until his thirst was satiated

scion = child, descendent
USE = He's the scion of a very wealthy family

scrupulous = principled, fastidious
USE = A scrupulous politician

sedentary = stationary, inactive
USE = sedentary lifestyle

serpentine = winding
USE = the serpentine course of the river

sonorous = resonant, majestic
USE = a sonorous voice

spurious = false, counterfeit
USE = spurious liquor

squander = waste
USE = They'll quite happily squander a whole year's savings on two-week vacation

stagnant = stale, motionless
USE = stagnant sales

stalwart = pillar, strong
USE = a stalwart supporter

stint = limit, assignment
USE = He has just finished a stint of compulsory military service

stipend = payment, allowance
USE = During summer project, he earned Rs 2,000 as stipend

stringent = severe, strict
USE = stringent laws

subjugate = to conquer
USE = India was subjugated by the British for hundreds of years

subsequent = succeeding, following
USE = The book discusses his illness and subsequent resignation from the government

sumptuous = opulent, luscious, lavish
USE = sumptuous meal

supersede = replace
USE = this agreement supersedes all old agreements

surfeit = overabundance
USE = India has a surfeit of cheap labor

surpass = exceed, excel
USE = your success will surpass your friend's expectations

susceptible = vulnerable
USE = children are susceptible to diseases

synthesis = combination
USE = a synthesis of what is best in India and America

tacit = understood without being spoken
USE = tacit understanding

tactile = tangible
USE = a tactile quality

terrestrial = earthly
USE = terrestrial rights

tome = large book
USE = a tome on the subject

topography = science of map making
USE = *

tractable = docile, manageable
USE = The problem turned out to be rather less tractable than I had expected

transpire = happen
USE = No one is willing to predict what may transpire at the peace conference

truncate = shorten
USE = TV coverage of the match was truncated by a technical fault

ubiquitous = omnipresent, pervasive
USE = the ubiquitous denim jeans

unanimity = agreement
USE = it was a rare decision made with unanimity

unconscionable = unscrupulous
USE = They both drank an unconscionable quantity of wine in the party

undermine = weaken
USE = Criticism just undermines their confidence

unequivocal = absolute, certain
USE = unequivocal support

unimpeachable = beyond question
USE = a man of unimpeachable integrity and character

untoward = perverse
USE = untoward happening

unwitting = unintentional
USE = unwitting victims of

urbane = refined, worldly
USE = an urbane, kindly and generous woman

utopia = perfect place
USE = the place is a kind of utopia

validate = affirm
USE = validate a claim

verbatim = Word for word
USE = She had an amazing memory and could recall verbatim quite complex conversations

verbose = Wordy
USE = a verbose explanation

vernacular = everyday language used by ordinary people
USE = the vernacular press

viable = capable of surviving
USE = viable solution

virtuoso = highly skilled artist
USE = Ravi Shankar is a virtuoso sitar player

vivacious = lively
USE = a vivacious person

volatile = unstable, explosive
USE = volatile temper

voracious = hungry
USE = a voracious reader

vulnerable = susceptible, innocent
USE = I felt very vulnerable, standing there in snow without warm clothes on

waive = forego
USE = The bank manager waived the charge

wanton = lewd, abandoned
USE = a wanton disregard for safety

windfall = bonus, boon, sudden
USE = windfall profits

xenophobia = fear or hatred of foreigners
USE = I found no xenophobia in America

zealot = fanatic
USE = a religious zealot

zenith = summit, highest point
USE = at the zenith of his achievement

CD 3

amulet = ornament worn as a charm against evil spirits, talisman
USE = many people in villages wear amulets

analogous = similar, comparable, parallel
USE = Hypnotic trance is in a sense analogous to sleep

anarchy = absence of government or law
USE = there was anarchy after the government fell

animosity = dislike, hatred
USE = animosity between the teams

antipathy = repulsion, hatred
USE = He is a private man with a deep antipathy towards the press

apathy = indifference, lack of emotion
USE = the government's apathy during the accident was shocking

aperture = opening
USE = aperture of the camera

appease = pacify, satisfy
USE = they changed the law in order to appease their critics

append = affix, attach
USE = append a short footnote to the text

apprise = inform, to give notice of
USE = The President has been apprised of the situation

arbitrary = tyrannical, capricious, depending solely on individual will
USE = an arbitrary decision

arcane = secret
USE = the arcane details of the agreement

arduous = extremely difficult, hard
USE = an arduous journey

arid = dry, dull
USE = an arid climate

articulate = well-spoken
USE = an articulate speech

ascertain = discover, determine, make certain of
USE = to ascertain the cause of

ascetic = a self-denying, simple person
USE = Gandhiji lived as an ascetic

astral = pertaining to stars, exalted, elevated in position
USE = astral body

astute = wise
USE = politically astute

atrophy = the wasting away of muscle
USE = After months in a hospital bed, his leg muscles had atrophied

attenuate = weaken, to make thin or slender
USE = Radiation from the sun is attenuated by the Earth's atmosphere

attest = testify
USE = attested copy of mark sheet

augment = increase, expand, extend
USE = He would have to find work to augment his income

auspicious = favorable, promising
USE = auspicious start

austere = stern, strict, unadorned, harsh, Spartan
USE = an austere room

autonomous = Self-governing, separate, independent
USE = an autonomous university

auxiliary = secondary, supplementary, reserve
USE = an auxiliary nurse

avarice = greed
USE = Her business empire brought her wealth beyond the dreams of avarice.

averse = loath, reluctant, being disinclined towards something
USE = the actor was not averse to giving interviews

avert = turn away
USE = avert a crisis

balm = soothing ointment, soothing, healing influence
USE = a new skin balm

belabor (BRITISH = belabour) = to assail verbally, to insist repeatedly or harp on
USE = belabor a point

belated = delayed, overdue, late
USE = Belated birthday greetings

belittle = disparage, to represent as unimportant
USE = they attempted to belittle the leader

bellicose = Warlike, aggressive
USE = a bellicose situation

belligerent = combative, hostile
USE = his assistant was belligerent

benefactor = patron, someone giving aid or money
USE = king Ashoka was a benefactor

benign = kind, gentle, or harmless
USE = a benign ruler or benign tumor

boisterous = rowdy, loud, noisy, unrestrained
USE = a boisterous child

brevity = shortness of expression
USE = brevity in writing is an art

buttress = support
USE = *

cacophony = dissonance, harsh noise
USE = a cacophony of voices

calamity = disaster
USE = natural calamity

callous = insensitive, thick-skinned
USE = callous attitude

capacious = spacious, large, roomy, extensive
USE = a capacious handbag

capitulate = to surrender, submit completely
USE = the enemy capitulated

caustic = biting, sarcastic, able to burn, scathing
USE = caustic remarks

censure = condemn, criticize or find fault with
USE = His dishonest behavior came under severe censure

champion = to defend or support
USE = an Olympic champion

charlatan = quack, fake
USE = the charlatan was caught

circuitous = roundabout
USE = a circuitous route

clandestine = secret
USE = clandestine activities

claustrophobia = fear of enclosed places
USE = He suffers from claustrophobia so he never travels on underground trains

collateral = securities for a debt, or accompanying
USE = She used her house as collateral for a loan

colloquial = informal speech
USE = colloquial speech

commensurate = proportionate
USE = a salary that is commensurate with skills and experience

complacent = self-satisfied, smug, affable
USE = students shouldn't become complacent about studies

compliant = submissive and yielding
USE = a compliant child

concatenate = link, linked together
USE = *

concave = curving inward
USE = a concave lens

conciliatory = reconciling, overcoming distrust or hostility
USE = a conciliatory approach

concomitant = accompanying something, concurrent
USE = Loss of memory is a natural concomitant of old age

condone = overlook wrong doing, pardon, justify
USE = If the government is seen to condone violence, the bloodshed will never stop

conduit = pipe, tube
USE = a conduit for water to flow through

confiscate = seize, to appropriate
USE = the government confiscated the criminal's property

congenial = friendly, similar in tastes and habits
USE = a congenial company

congenital = inborn, existing from birth
USE = a congenital disease

conjugal = pertaining to marriage
USE = conjugal happiness

connoisseur = an expert, gourmet, a person with refined taste
USE = a connoisseur of art

conscientious = honorable, upright, careful and thorough
USE = a conscientious student

consensus = general agreement, unanimity of opinion
USE = to reach a consensus

consonant = harmonious, in agreement with
USE = *

consummate = perfect, having great skills, complete, accomplished
USE = a consummate professional

contentious = argumentative, quarrelsome, disagreeable, belligerent
USE = a contentious decision

contravene = oppose, to contradict, deny, act contrary to
USE = by accepting the money, she was in contravention of company rules.

convene = assemble (a group), to meet, come together
USE = the committee convenes three times a year

conventional = customary, standard, typical, commonplace
USE = a conventional wedding

convex = curving outward
USE = convex mirror

convoluted = twisted, complicated, involved
USE = a very convoluted route

copious = abundant, plentiful
USE = they drank copious amounts of wine

countermand = overrule, to annual, cancel
USE = the general countermanded the orders issued in his absence

covert = secret, hidden
USE = covert police operations

crescendo = becoming louder, gradual increase in volume of sound
USE = The music reached a crescendo.

criterion = a standard used in judging, rule for testing
USE = judged by financial criteria alone

cryptic = mysterious, puzzling
USE = a cryptic message

cursory = hasty, superficial
USE = a cursory glance

curtail = to shorten
USE = to curtain spending

dearth = scarcity, lack, insufficiency
USE = there is no dearth of talent in the country

debilitate = to weaken, enfeeble
USE = Chemotherapy exhausted and debilitated him

definitive = conclusive, final, clear-cut, explicit or decisive
USE = a definitive judgment

demise = Death
USE = demise of her mother

denounce = condemn, to accuse, blame
USE = they've been denounced as terrorists

depict = portray, to describe, represent
USE = Her paintings depict the lives of ordinary people

deplete = exhaust, to use up
USE = Alcohol depletes the body of B vitamins

deplore = condemn, to express or feel disapproval of, regret strongly
USE = a deplorable situation

deploy = arrange forces, to spread out strategically over an area
USE = to deploy my skills

destitute = very poor, poverty-stricken
USE = The floods left thousands of people destitute

detached = emotionally removed, separate, unconnected
USE = She seemed a bit detached, as if her mind were on other things

detrimental = harmful or injury
USE = a detrimental effect

deviate = turn away from, to stray, wander
USE = The recent pattern of weather deviates from the norm for this time of year

devoid = empty, totally lacking
USE = devoid of all comforts

devout = pious, deeply religious
USE = a devout Hindu

diabolical = devilish, fiendish, wicked
USE = Conditions in the prison were diabolical

diaphanous = sheer, translucent, allowing light to show through, delicate
USE = a diaphanous silk veil

dictum = popular saying, authoritative statement
USE = He followed the famous American dictum, 'Don't get mad, get even'

digress = ramble, to turn aside, to stray from the main point
USE = don't digress from the topic

dilapidated = neglected, in disrepair, run-down
USE = dilapidated buildings

dilate = enlarge, swell, extend
USE = dilated pupils

disarray = disorder, clutter
USE = The news threw his plans into disarray

disclaim = renounce, to deny, disavow
USE = the terrorists disclaimed responsibility for the bomb blast

discrepancy = difference between
USE = There is some discrepancy between the two accounts

dispassionate = Impartial, free from emotion, unbiased
USE = clear-sighted and dispassionate

disperse = scatter, to break up
USE = to disperse the crowd

dissemble = pretend, disguise one's motives
USE = He accused the government of dissembling

disseminate = distribute, to spread far and wide
USE = web sites are used to disseminate political propaganda

dissuade = to persuade someone to alter original intentions
USE = We tried to dissuade him from leaving.

diverge = branch off, to move in different directions
USE = their paths diverged

diverse = varying, differing
USE = unity in diversity

divest = strip, deprive, to get rid of
USE = The company is divesting its less profitable business operations

dogmatic = certain, unchanging in opinion
USE = a dogmatic approach to life

doldrums = dullness
USE = Her career was in the doldrums

dormant = asleep, at rest, inactive
USE = a dormant volcano

effigy = likeness, mannequin
USE = Crowds marched through the streets carrying burning effigies of the president

egregious = grossly wrong
USE = an egregious example of racism

egress = exit
USE = everyone rushed to the egress

emancipate = liberate
USE = emancipated women

embellish = exaggerate, make attractive with decoration
USE = He embellished the story with lots of dramatic details.

eminent = distinguished, famous, celebrated
USE = an eminent scientist

emulate = imitate
USE = emulate the success of others

enormity = large, tragic, state of being gigantic or terrible
USE = enormity of the situation

entice = to lure or tempt
USE = entice the customer into buying things

ephemeral = short-lived, momentary, fleeting
USE = his fame was ephemeral

equanimity = composure, calmness
USE = he replied with equanimity

equitable = fair
USE = a fair and equitable voting system

equivocate = make intentionally ambiguous
USE = She accused the minister of equivocating

erratic = constantly changing
USE = erratic power supply

erroneous = mistaken, in error
USE = an erroneous answer

erudite = learned
USE = erudite guest

esoteric = known by only a few
USE = an esoteric collection

ethereal = light, airy, spiritual, delicate
USE = ethereal beauty

etymology = study of words
USE = an interest in etymology

euphemism = genteel expression
USE = Passed away" is a euphemism for "died

evoke = draw forth, to produce a reaction
USE = evoke memories of childhood

exorbitant = expensive, greater than reasonable
USE = exorbitant prices

explicit = definite, clear
USE = explicit about one's plans

extort = extract, force
USE = to extort money

façade = mask, front, face
USE = the building has a new façade

facilitate = make easier, to aid, assist
USE = to facilitate the process

facsimile = duplicate
USE = facsimile machine is a fax machine

fallacious = wrong, unsound, illogical
USE = fallacious argument

fanaticism = excessive zeal, extreme devotion to a cause
USE = their fanaticism led to the fight

feasible = likely to succeed, possible
USE = a feasible plan

fiasco = debacle, disaster
USE = the dinner party was a complete fiasco

finesse = skill
USE = It was a disappointing performance which lacked finesse

foil = defeat
USE = The prisoners' attempt to escape was foiled

forensic = pertaining to debate, solving crime
USE = forensic evidence

frugal = thrifty
USE = a frugal millionaire

furor (BRITISH = furore) = commotion
USE = the furor over his last film

genteel = elegant
USE = genteel manners

grandiose = impressive, large
USE = grandiose ceremony

gratis = free, costing nothing
USE = I'll give it to you, gratis!

gratuitous = unwarranted, uncalled for, free
USE = gratuitous violence

gratuity = tip
USE = you give gratuity or tip to the waiter

gregarious = sociable, outgoing
USE = a gregarious person

gullible = easily deceived
USE = gullible people

homage = respect
USE = to pay homage

homogeneous = uniform
USE = homogeneous milk

humane = Compassionate
USE = humane treatment of prisoners of war

hyperbole = exaggeration
USE = The blurb on the back of the book was full of the usual hyperbole - 'enthralling', 'fascinating' and so on

iconoclast = on who attacks traditional beliefs
USE = he is an iconoclast

idiosyncrasy = peculiarity of temperament
USE = She often cracks her knuckles when she's speaking - it's one of her little idiosyncrasies.

ignoble = dishonorable
USE = an ignoble action

illusory = fleeting, unreal
USE = illusory statements

immaculate = spotlessly clean, free from error
USE = dressed immaculately

immobile = still, not moveable
USE = She sat immobile, wondering what to do next

immutable = Unchangeable
USE = immutable law

impasse = deadlock
USE = The dispute had reached an impasse, as neither side would compromise

impeach = accuse, charge
USE = The governor was impeached for wrongful use of state money

impediment = obstacle
USE = war is an impediment to progress of the country

implicit = Implied
USE = an implicit threat

impotent = powerless
USE = When your child is ill, you feel impotent

impromptu = spontaneous, without rehearsal
USE = impromptu speech

incarnate = having bodily form
USE = as devil's incarnate

incense = enrage
USE = I was so incensed by what he was saying I had to walk out.

incessant = Unceasing
USE = incessant rain

inclusive = comprehensive
USE = the price is inclusive of taxes

incongruous = out of place, absurd
USE = The new computer looked incongruous in the dark book-filled library

incorrigible = who cannot be reformed
USE = an incorrigible liar

incredulous = skeptical, doubtful
USE = incredulous spectators

induce = persuade, bring about
USE = They induced her to take the job by promising more money

inept = unfit, clumsy
USE = an inept comment

inert = inactive
USE = The dog lay inert on the sofa

inevitable = Unavoidable, predestined
USE = an inevitable war

infer = conclude, deduce
USE = What do you infer from her refusal?

infinitesimal = very small
USE = The amounts of radioactivity present were infinitesimal.

infringe = encroach
USE = They infringed building regulations

ingenious = clever
USE = ingenious solution to a difficult problem

initiate = begin, introduce
USE = initiate a discussion

inkling = A hint
USE = He must have had some inkling of what was happening

innate = inborn, natural
USE = his innate goodness

insatiable = never satisfied
USE = an insatiable appetite

insidious = treacherous, sly
USE = High-blood pressure is an insidious condition which has few symptoms

insolvent = bankrupt
USE = the company went insolent

instigate = incite, urge, agitate
USE = The government will instigate new measures to combat terrorism

integrate = make whole
USE = He seems to find it difficult to integrate socially

interpolate = insert
USE = interpolate the data

intractable = not easily managed
USE = an intractable problem

intrinsic = Inherent, internal
USE = intrinsic value

invalidate = disprove, to negate or nullify
USE = the new experiment invalidated the old theory

invincible = cannot be defeated, unbeatable
USE = Last year the company seemed invincible but in recent weeks has begun to have problems

irrevocable = cannot be rescinded, irreversible
USE = an irrevocable decision

itinerary = detailed plan or route of a journey
USE = The tour operator will arrange transport and plan your itinerary

jargon = specialized language
USE = computer jargon

jocular = humorous, playful
USE = a jocular comment

judicious = prudent, showing good judgment
USE = The letter was judiciously worded

juncture = point where two things are joined
USE = At this juncture

jurisprudence = philosophy of law
USE = a student of jurisprudence

kindle = arouse, inspire
USE = the exciting stories she read kindled her interest

kinetic = pertaining to motion
USE = kinetic energy

labyrinth = maze
USE = Finally, through a labyrinth of corridors she found his office

laconic = brief, terse, using few words
USE = She had a laconic wit

laggard = lazy person, slow, or old-fashioned
USE = laggards are the last ones to accept any change

lascivious = Lustful, lewd
USE = a lascivious smile

lassitude = lethargy
USE = they are blaming the company's problems on the lassitude of the managing director

latent = potential, present but hidden
USE = the latent artistic talents that many people possess

lavish = to give plentiful amounts of
USE = lavish gifts

libidinous = lustful
USE = they objected to his libidinous behavior

CD 4

exacerbate = worsen
USE = This attack will exacerbate the already tense relations between the two communities

exasperate = irritate, vex
USE = he often exasperates his mother with pranks

execrable = very bad, abominable, utterly detestable
USE = an execrable performance

exemplary = outstanding, serving as an example
USE = exemplary behavior

exhort = strongly urge
USE = The governor exhorted the prisoners not to riot

exhume = uncover, to remove from a grave
USE = his body was exhumed and an autopsy ordered

exonerate = free from blame
USE = The report exonerated the crew from all responsibility for the collision

exorcise = to expel evil spirits
USE = After the priest exorcized the house, apparently, the strange noises stopped

expedient = advantageous, convenient, efficient
USE = It might be expedient not to pay him until the work is finished

expiate = atone, make amends for
USE = to expiate a crime

expunge = erase, eliminate completely
USE = His name was expunged from the list of members

extenuate = To diminish the gravity or importance of
USE = He was unable to say anything that might have extenuated his behavior

extol = praise highly
USE = She is forever extolling the virtues of her children

extraneous = not essential, unnecessary
USE = extraneous information

extricate = Disentangle, free
USE = It took hours to extricate the car from the sand

exuberant = joyous, happy
USE = Young and exuberant

exude = emit, ooze
USE = She just exudes confidence

exult = rejoice
USE = She seems to exult in her power

facetious = joking, sarcastic, witty
USE = facetious remarks

facile = very easy
USE = a facile explanation

fallow = unproductive, unplowed
USE = a fallow period

fastidious = meticulous, careful with details
USE = He is very fastidious about how a suitcase should be packed

fathom = understand, to measure the depth of
USE = I find his novels impossible to fathom

fatuous = inane, stupid
USE = a fatuous idea

fealty = Loyalty
USE = the prime minister demanded fealty of his ministers

fecund = fertile, fruitful, productive
USE = fecund soil

feign = pretend, give a false impression
USE = to feign surprise

fetid = foul-smelling, putrid, stinking
USE = fetid air

fickle = always changing one's mind
USE = The world of popular music is notoriously fickle

fidelity = Loyalty
USE = marital fidelity

filch = steal something of little value
USE = Who's filched my pencils

filial = of a son or daughter
USE = filial affection

fitful = irregular
USE = a fitful sleep

flagrant = outrageous, shameless
USE = a flagrant misuse of funds

fledgling = just beginning, struggling
USE = fledgling businesses.

flippant = Having a light, pert, trifling disposition
USE = a flippant attitude

florid = ruddy, with too much decoration
USE = a florid architectural style

flout = to show disregard for the law or rules
USE = flout the law

foible = weakness, minor fault
USE = We all have our little foibles

foist = palm off a fake
USE = I try not to foist my values on the children but it's hard

foment = instigate
USE = The song was banned on the grounds that it might foment communal tension

fortuitous = happening by luck, fortunate
USE = fortuitous gains

foster = encourage
USE = to foster an interest in

fracas = noisy fight
USE = He was injured in a fracas outside a disco

fraught = filled
USE = fraught with risks

frenetic = harried, neurotic
USE = frenetic activity

frond = bending tree
USE = Ferns and palms have fronds

fulminate = denounce, menace
USE = to fulminate against the government

fulsome = excessive, insincere
USE = Her new book has received fulsome praise from the critics

furtive = stealthy
USE = He made one or two furtive phone calls

gainsay = to deny
USE = there's no gainsaying the technical brilliance of his performance

gargantuan = large
USE = a gargantuan appetite

garner = gather
USE = to garner several awards

garrulous = talkative, loquacious, wordy
USE = the garrulous old gentleman

gauche = awkward, crude
USE = a gauche teenager

genre = kind, category
USE = a literary genre

gibe = heckle
USE = She gibed constantly at the way he ran his business

glib = insincere manner
USE = No one was convinced by his glib answers

glower = stare angrily
USE = There's no point glowering at me like that

goad = encourage
USE = He refused to be goaded by their insults

gossamer = thin and flimsy
USE = a gossamer veil

gouge = overcharge, scoop out
USE = the enemy gouged out his eyes

grimace = expression of disgust
USE = grimace with pain

grovel = crawl, obey
USE = a groveling note of apology

guile = deceit, trickery
USE = He is a simple, honest man, totally lacking in guile

hackneyed = trite
USE = The plot of the film is just a hackneyed boy-meets-girl scenario

hapless = unlucky
USE = hapless victims of war

harangue = a pompous speech
USE = A drunk in the station was haranguing passers-by

harbinger = forerunner
USE = a harbinger of doom

haughty = arrogant
USE = a haughty manner

hedonism = the pursuit of pleasure in life
USE = hedonism vs. asceticism

heinous = shocking, wicked
USE = heinous crime

hermetic = airtight, sealed
USE = a hermetic seal

hew = to cut with an ax
USE = The monument was hewn out of the side of a mountain

hiatus = interruption
USE = to resume production after a two-month hiatus

hone = sharpen
USE = Her debating skills were honed in the students' union

illimitable = limitless
USE = illimitable space

imbue = infuse, dye, wet
USE = His poetry is imbued with religious feelings

immure = build a wall around
USE = the student immured himself in the room for two weeks before exams

impair = injure
USE = A recurring knee injury might have impaired his chances of winning the tournament

impassive = calm, without feeling
USE = an impassive individual

impeccable = faultless
USE = His English is impeccable

impecunious = indigent, having no money
USE = an impecunious student

imperious = domineering
USE = an imperious manner

impertinent = insolent, rude
USE = an impertinent question

imperturbable = calm
USE = he remained imperturbable despite the panic around him

impervious = Impenetrable
USE = How does glue bond with impervious substances like glass and metal

impetuous = quick to act without thinking
USE = He's so impetuous - why can't he think things over before he rushes into them

implausible = unlikely, inconceivable
USE = The whole plot of the film is ridiculously implausible

impolitic = unwise
USE = I thought it impolitic to ask any questions about her child's failure

importune = urgent request
USE = As a tourist, you are importuned for money the moment you step outside your hotel

impregnable = totally safe from attack
USE = Despite burglar alarms, homes are never impregnable against determined thieves

impugn = criticize
USE = Are you impugning my competence as a professional designer

inadvertent = unintentional
USE = All authors need to be wary of inadvertent copying of other people's ideas

inane = vacuous, stupid
USE = There are too many inane quiz shows on television these days

incandescent = brilliant
USE = incandescent bulb

incarcerate = to put in a jail
USE = Thousands of dissidents have been incarcerated

incendiary = burning easily, flammable
USE = an incendiary bomb

inchoate = just begun
USE = She had a child's inchoate awareness of language

incipient = beginning to exist
USE = signs of incipient public frustration

incisive = keen, penetrating
USE = incisive questions

incognito = disguised
USE = The prince often traveled abroad incognito

incommunicado = unable to communicate with others
USE = His secretary says he will be incommunicado for the rest of the day

incontrovertible = Indisputable
USE = incontrovertible proof

inculcate = instill, indoctrinate, to teach
USE = to inculcate a team spirit

incumbent = obligatory, required
USE = She felt it incumbent upon her

incursion = raid
USE = incursions into enemy territory

indict = charge with a crime
USE = Five people were indicted for making and selling counterfeit currency

indigenous = Native
USE = Are there any species of frog indigenous to the area

indigent = very poor
USE = *

indolent = lazy
USE = an indolent reply

indomitable = invincible, fearless
USE = The indomitable Mr. Gandhi said he would continue to fight for justice

indubitable = unquestionable
USE = an indubitable fact

inexorable = relentless, inflexible
USE = the inexorable progress of science

infallible = incapable of making a mistake
USE = Even the experts are not infallible

infernal = hellish
USE = He described a journey through the infernal world

infirmity = ailment, disease
USE = an advanced state of infirmity

ingrate = ungrateful person
USE = *

ingratiate = pleasing, flattering, endearing
USE = He's always trying to ingratiate himself with his boss

inimical = adverse, hostile, unfriendly
USE = Excessive managerial control is inimical to creative expression

innocuous = Harmless
USE = Some mushrooms look innocuous but are in fact poisonous

innuendo = indirect and subtle criticism
USE = an element of sexual innuendo

inscrutable = cannot be fully understood
USE = an inscrutable face

insinuate = to suggest, imply, say indirectly
USE = Are you insinuating I'm losing my nerve?

insipid = flat, dull, lacking flavor
USE = He's an insipid old bore.

insolent = insulting
USE = an insolent gesture

insular = narrow-minded, isolated
USE = insular ideas

insuperable = insurmountable
USE = insuperable difficulties

insurgent = rebellious
USE = All approaches to the capital are now under the control of the insurgents

insurrection = uprising, rebellion
USE = armed insurrection

inter = bury
USE = Many of the soldiers were interred in unmarked graves

interdict = prohibit
USE = all nations must interdict the use of nuclear weapons

interloper = intruder, meddler in others' affairs
USE = Security did not prevent an interloper from entering

interminable = unending
USE = an interminable delay

internecine = mutually destructive
USE = internecine war

intransigent = uncompromising
USE = an intransigent position

intrepid = fearless
USE = a team of intrepid explorers

inundate = flood
USE = We have been inundated with requests for help

invective = verbal insult
USE = A stream of invective from some sectors of the press continues to assail the government

inveigh = to rail against, protest strongly
USE = There were politicians who inveighed against immigrants to get votes

inveterate = habitual, chronic, long-standing
USE = I never trust anything he says - the man's an inveterate liar

invidious = incurring ill-will
USE = Such a difficult choice placed her in an invidious position

irascible = irritable
USE = She's becoming more and more irascible as she grows older

itinerant = Wandering, unsettled
USE = an itinerant journalist

jaded = spent, bored with one's situation
USE = jaded palate

juggernaut = unstoppable force
USE = nothing could survive in the path of juggernaut

kismet = fate
USE = this is my kismet

knell = sound of a funeral bell
USE = toll the death knell

lachrymose = tearful
USE = lachrymose movies

lampoon = satirize, to attack with satire
USE = merciless political lampoons

larceny = theft of property
USE = he was charged with grand larceny

largess = generous donation
USE = beneficiary of the millionaire's largesse

legerdemain = trickery
USE = the magician demonstrated his legerdemain

levity = Frivolity, humor
USE = a brief moment of levity amid the solemn proceedings

libertine = one without moral restraint
USE = he had the reputation as a libertine

licentious = lewd, immoral
USE = *

limpid = transparent, clearly understood
USE = a limpid pool; limpid prose

lissome (BRITISH = lissom) = agile, supple
USE = lissome and graceful

lithe = moving and bending with ease
USE = He had the lithe, athletic body of a ballet dancer

loathe = abhor, hate
USE = I loathe doing housework

loquacious = Talkative
USE = she is very loquacious

lugubrious = sad, sorrowful
USE = a lugubrious face

lurid = glowing, shocking
USE = You can read all the lurid details of the affair in today's paper

macabre = gruesome
USE = macabre nature of the killing

machination = plot or scheme
USE = I can see through your wily machination

maelstrom = whirlpool, agitated state of mind
USE = the maelstrom of civil war

malapropism = comical misuse of a word
USE = *

malcontent = one who is forever dissatisfied
USE = he was one of the few malcontent in the congress

malediction = curse
USE = the witch uttered malediction against her captors

malefactor = evildoer, culprit
USE = try to bring the malefactors to justice

malodorous = fetid, foul-smelling
USE = a malodorous swamp

manifold = multiple, diverse
USE = Despite her manifold faults, she was a strong leader

martial = warlike, pertaining to the military
USE = Kung fu and karate are martial arts

martinet = strict disciplinarian
USE = the officer was a martinet

masochist = one who enjoys pain
USE = I say you need to be a masochist to run marathons

maudlin = weepy, sentimental
USE = I don't like such maudlin pictures

maverick = a person who resists adherence to a group
USE = a political maverick

mawkish = sickeningly sentimental
USE = The film lapses into mawkish sentimentality near the end

meander = to wander aimlessly without direction
USE = The film meanders along with no particular story line

mendicant = beggar
USE = mendicants and peddlers

mercurial = changeable, volatile, quick
USE = a mercurial temperament

mettle = courage, capacity for bravery
USE = The Indian athletes proved their mettle in the final round

minatory = threatening
USE = all abusive or minatory letters

mirth = jollity, laughter
USE = Her jokes were a source of considerable mirth

miscreant = one who behaves criminally
USE = We need tougher penalties to discourage miscreants

missive = letter or note
USE = a ten-page missive

modicum = a small amount
USE = a modicum of truth

mollify = to calm or make less severe
USE = I tried to mollify her by giving her flowers

moot = disputable, previously decided
USE = It's a moot point

mordant = biting, sarcastic
USE = mordant humor

mores = moral standards, customs
USE = middle-class mores

moribund = near death
USE = How can the shopping mall be revived from its present moribund state?

mote = speck, small particle
USE = the tiniest mote in the eye is very painful

motley = diverse, many colored
USE = a motley collection of old furniture

multifarious = diverse, many-sided
USE = his multifarious business activities

munificent = generous
USE = donated a munificent sum of money

myriad = innumerable
USE = a myriad of choices

nascent = incipient, coming into existence
USE = a nascent problem

natal = related to birth
USE = pre-natal medicine

necromancy = sorcery, black magic
USE = feats of necromancy

Nemesis = implacable foe, often victorious opponent
USE = The tax increases proved to be the Prime Minister's political nemesis at the following election

neologism = new word or expression
USE = *

neophyte = beginner
USE = experts as well as neophytes

nether = located under or below
USE = building's nether regions

nettle = irritate
USE = She looked up at me sharply, clearly nettled by the interruption

niggardly = stingy
USE = a niggardly donation

noisome = harmful, stinking
USE = a noisome stench

nonentity = person of no significance
USE = a political nonentity

obdurate = unyielding
USE = The President remains obdurate on the question of tax cuts

obeisance = homage, deference
USE = One by one the noblemen made their obeisance to the Queen

obfuscate = bewilder, muddle, to confuse
USE = arguments that obfuscated the main issue

oblique = indirect
USE = He gave her an oblique glance

obliterate = destroy
USE = The missile strike was devastating - the target was totally obliterated

obloquy = slander, abusive language
USE = to cast obloquy on someone's reputation

obsequious = fawning, servile, overly submissive
USE = He is almost embarrassingly obsequious to anyone in authority

obsequy = funeral ceremony
USE = hundreds of people paid their last respects at the obsequies.

obstinate = stubborn
USE = her obstinate refusal to compromise

obstreperous = noisy, unruly, troublesome
USE = obstreperous customers

obtuse = stupid, dull
USE = are you being deliberately obtuse

occlude = block, to shut
USE = a blood clot occluded an artery to the heart

odious = despicable, hateful
USE = an odious crime

onerous = burdensome
USE = the onerous task of finding a peaceful solution

opprobrious = abusive, disgraceful
USE = opprobrious conduct

ordain = appoint
USE = ordained as a priest

ossify = harden
USE = Years of easy success had ossified the company's thinking and it never faced up to the challenge of the new technology

ostensible = apparent, seeming
USE = ostensible goal

ostentatious = pretentious, showy
USE = an ostentatious gesture

overweening = arrogant, forward
USE = overweening ambition

CD 5

pacifist = one who opposes all violence
USE = The pacifist movement

paean = a song of praise
USE = The song is a paean to solitude and independence

palaver = babble, nonsense
USE = the task was such a palaver, I swore I'd never do it again

pall = to become dull or weary
USE = work quickly palled

palliate = to make less serious, ease
USE = doctors must palliate which they can't cure

pallid = pale, sallow, lacking color or liveliness
USE = His face seemed pallid and unhealthy

palpable = touchable, obvious, real
USE = a palpable effect

paltry = scarce, pitifully small or worthless
USE = a paltry sum

panache = flamboyance, flair
USE = He dressed with panache.

pandemic = spread over a whole area or country
USE = Malaria is still pandemic in India

panegyric = praise
USE = She delivered a panegyric on the President-elect

panoply = full suit of armor
USE = panoply of remedies and drugs

paragon = model of excellence or perfection
USE = a paragon of virtue

pariah = outcast
USE = I am not a pariah to be shunned and outcast

parley = conference, discussion
USE = After some serious parleying, both sides agreed to settle their differences

parry = avert, ward off, reflect
USE = the president parried enquiries about the arms scandal

partisan = supporter
USE = partisan politics

pathos = emotion, feeling of sadness
USE = There's a pathos in his writings

patrician = aristocrat
USE = we greatly admired her well-bred, patrician elegance

patrimony = inheritance or heritage derived from one's father
USE = he spent his patrimony within two years of his father's death

peccadillo = a minor fault
USE = a youthful peccadillo

pedagogue = dull, formal teacher
USE = *

pedant = a person who is too interested in formal rules and small unimportant details
USE = *

pejorative = insulting, having bad connotations
USE = an unflattering or pejorative word

pellucid = transparent, easily understood
USE = students liked the teachers' pellucid style

penance = voluntary suffering to repent for a wrong
USE = They are doing penance for their sins

penchant = inclination
USE = a penchant for exotic clothes

penitent = repentant
USE = a penitent smile

pensive = sad
USE = She became withdrawn and pensive

perdition = damnation, complete ruin
USE = eternal perdition

peremptory = dictatorial
USE = He started issuing peremptory instructions

perennial = enduring, lasting
USE = The Taj Mahal is a perennial tourist favorite

perfidious = treacherous (of a person)
USE = a perfidious attack on democracy

perfunctory = careless, done in a routine way
USE = Her smile was perfunctory.

peripatetic = moving from place to place
USE = a peripatetic music teacher

pernicious = destructive
USE = The cuts in government funding had a pernicious effect on local health services

pert = flippant, bold
USE = a pert answer

pertinacious = persevering
USE = Like most successful politicians, she is pertinacious and single-minded in the pursuit of her goals

pertinent = Relevant, applicable
USE = a pertinent question

philistine = barbarian, narrow-minded person
USE = a bunch of philistines

phlegmatic = sluggish, someone who is calm
USE = As a footballer his great asset was his calm, phlegmatic manner

pillory = punish by ridicule
USE = Although regularly pilloried by the press as an obnoxious loudmouth, he is, nonetheless, an effective politician

pique = sting, arouse interest
USE = He stormed from the room in a fit of pique, shouting that he had been misunderstood

pithy = concise, to the point
USE = a pithy orange

pittance = alms, trifle
USE = He works hard but he's paid a pittance.

placid = Serene, calm
USE = a slow-moving and placid river

platitude = trite remark, stale
USE = The captain doesn't mouth platitudes about it not mattering who scores as long as the team wins

plebeian = common, vulgar
USE = He retained a plebeian taste in food and drink

plethora = overabundance
USE = a plethora of books about

poignant = pungent, sharp, emotionally moving
USE = It is especially poignant that he died on the day before the wedding

polemic = a controversy
USE = a fierce anti-war polemic

portend = omen
USE = to portend the end of the world

portly = large, dignified
USE = a portly figure

potentate = sovereign, king
USE = the potentate spent more time playing music than governing the country

prattle = chatter, foolish talk
USE = Stop your prattling and go to sleep

precept = principle, law
USE = This policy goes against common precepts of decency

precipice = cliff, edge
USE = The film opens with a shot of a climber dangling from a precipice

precipitous = steep
USE = a precipitous mountain path

precocious = advanced
USE = A precocious child, she went to university at the age of 15

precursor = forerunner
USE = Sulfur dioxide is the main precursor of acid rain

predilection = inclination, preference
USE = a predilection for spicy food

premeditate = plan in advance
USE = a premeditated murder

preponderance = predominance
USE = preponderance of evidence

preposterous = ridiculous, illogical
USE = a preposterous suggestion

presage = omen, indicate in advance
USE = the economy is not showing signs of any of the excesses that normally presage a recession

privation = lack of usual necessities or comforts
USE = Economic privation is pushing the poor towards crime

probity = integrity, complete honesty
USE = Her probity and integrity are beyond question

proclivity = inclination, tendency
USE = his proclivity for

prodigal = wasteful
USE = he has been prodigal with company funds

prodigious = marvelous, enormous
USE = a prodigious musician

profligate = licentious, prodigal, corrupt
USE = She is well-known for her profligate spending habits

progenitor = ancestor
USE = Marx was the progenitor of communism

progeny = children
USE = His numerous progeny are scattered all over the country

prognosis = forecast
USE = The prognosis after the operation was for a full recovery

prognosticate = foretell
USE = I prognosticate disaster unless we change our wasteful ways

prolix = long-winded, wordy
USE = The author's prolix style has done nothing to encourage sales of the book

promontory = headland, cape
USE = a lighthouse on the promontory

promulgate = publish, disseminate
USE = The new law was finally promulgated

propensity = inclination
USE = a propensity to talk too much

propinquity = nearness, kinship
USE = their relationship was not based on mere propinquity, they were true friends

propitiate = satisfy, to win over
USE = In those days people might sacrifice a goat or sheep to propitiate an angry god

propitious = auspicious, favorable
USE = the most propitious time to start up a company

prosaic = uninspired, flat, dull
USE = He asked if I'd got my black eye in a fight - I told him the prosaic truth that I'd banged my head on a door

proscribe = prohibit, to condemn
USE = The Athletics Federation have banned the runner from future races for using proscribed drugs

proselytize (BRITISH = proselytise) = recruit, convert
USE = the proselytizing zeal

protean = changing readily
USE = the protean talents of this comedian

protract = To prolong, extend
USE = I have no desire to protract the process

provident = having foresight, thrifty
USE = provident fund

prude = puritan
USE = Don't be such a prude.

prudent = cautious, careful
USE = It's always prudent to

prurient = exhibiting lewd desires
USE = He denied that the article had been in any way prurient

puerile = Childish
USE = I find his sense of humor rather puerile

pugnacious = combative, quarrelsome
USE = I found him pugnacious and arrogant

pulchritude = beauty
USE = female pulchritude

punctilious = careful in observing rules of behavior or ceremony
USE = He was always punctilious in his manners

pungent = sharp smell or taste
USE = the pungent whiff of a goat

purport = claim to be
USE = They purport to represent the wishes of the majority of parents at the school

pusillanimous = cowardly
USE = He's too pusillanimous to stand up to his opponents

quaff = to drink heartily
USE = as they quaffed their wine, they listened to old songs

quagmire = difficult situation
USE = to sink deeper into a quagmire

quandary = dilemma, difficulty
USE = I've had two job offers, and I'm in a real quandary about which one to accept

quell = suppress, allay
USE = to quell the disturbances

querulous = complaining
USE = He became increasingly dissatisfied and querulous in his old age

quibble = to argue about insignificant and irrelevant details
USE = There's no point quibbling over five Rupees

quiescent = still, motionless, at rest
USE = relatively quiescent

Quixotic = impractical, romantic
USE = This is a vast, exciting and some say quixotic project

raconteur = story teller
USE = a brilliant raconteur

rampant = unbridled, raging
USE = rampant corruption

rancor (BRITISH = rancour) = resentment, dislike
USE = They cheated me, but I feel no rancor towards them

rant = rage, scold
USE = He's always ranting about the government

rapacious = grasping, avaricious, greedy
USE = her rapacious appetite for fame

rapprochement = reconciliation
USE = rapprochement between the warring factions

raze = destroy
USE = The town was razed to the ground

recalcitrant = resisting authority or control
USE = zebras are reputed to be the most recalcitrant of animals

recant = retract a statement
USE = After a year spent in solitary confinement, he publicly recanted

recidivism = habitual criminal activity
USE = *

recondite = known to only a few
USE = complex and recondite

recreant = coward, betrayer of faith
USE = the religious people ostracized the recreant who had abandoned their faith

refractory = obstinate
USE = the refractory horse was removed from the race

regal = royal
USE = a regal manner

relegate = assign to an inferior position
USE = She resigned when she was relegated to a desk job

renege = break a promise
USE = If you renege on the deal now, I'll fight you in the courts

replete = complete
USE = This car has an engine replete with the latest technology

reprehensible = blameworthy, unacceptable
USE = reprehensible conduct

reproach = blame
USE = You have nothing to reproach yourself for

reprobate = morally unprincipled person
USE = Every time I see you, you're drunk, you old reprobate

reprove = to criticize or correct
USE = The teacher gently reproved the boys for not paying attention

repudiate = to reject as having no authority
USE = He repudiated the allegation

requiem = rest, a mass for the dead
USE = Mozart's Requiem

requite = to return in kind
USE = Requited love is not enough to sustain a long-term relationship

rescind = revoke, cancel
USE = The new policy proved unpopular and was rescinded

respite = interval or relief
USE = We worked for hours without respite

resplendent = shining, splendid
USE = the queen's resplendent purple robes

restitution = act of compensating for loss or damage
USE = The chemicals company promised to make full restitution to the victims for the injury to their health

restive = nervous, uneasy
USE = The audience was becoming restive as they waited for the performance to begin

retort = quick replay
USE = "That doesn't concern you!" she retorted.

retrench = reorganize, to regroup
USE = The company had to retrench because of falling orders

retrieve = reclaim
USE = We taught our dog to retrieve a ball

retrograde = regress
USE = a retrograde step

revelry = merrymaking
USE = Sounds of revelry came from next door

revere = honor
USE = Nelson Mandela is revered for his brave fight against apartheid

revile = to criticize with harsh language
USE = The judge was reviled in the newspapers for his opinions on the capital punishment

revulsion = aversion
USE = turned away in revulsion

ribald = coarse, vulgar
USE = He entertained us with his ribald stories

rife = widespread, abundant
USE = Dysentery and malaria are rife in the refugee camps

risque = off-color, racy
USE = risque anecdotes

rostrum = stage for public speaking
USE = the new speaker arrived at the rostrum and started speaking

ruminate = reflect upon
USE = She ruminated for weeks about whether to tell him or not

rustic = rural
USE = a rustic bench

sacrosanct = sacred
USE = I'm willing to help on any weekday, but I'm afraid my weekends are sacrosanct

sagacious = wise
USE = a sagacious person

sallow = sickly yellow in color
USE = a sallow complexion

sanguine = cheerful
USE = They are less sanguine about the prospects for peace

sapient = wise, shrewd
USE = the students enjoyed professor's sapient digressions more than his formal lectures

sardonic = scornful
USE = a sardonic smile

saunter = walk in a leisurely manner
USE = He sauntered by, looking very pleased with himself

savant = scholar
USE = world famous savants

schism = a division or separation
USE = a schism within the Church

scintilla = very small amount
USE = There's not a scintilla of truth in what he says

scintillate = sparkle
USE = I enjoyed the party because the food was good and conversation scintillating

scoff = ridicule
USE = The critics scoffed at his paintings

scurrilous = abusive, insulting
USE = a scurrilous remark

secular = worldly, nonreligious
USE = secular education

sedition = treason, resistance to authority
USE = his words were calculated to arouse sedition

sententious = concise, trying to appear wise
USE = sententious and pompous

sequester = to remove or set apart
USE = he hopes to sequester himself in a small community

seraphic = angelic, pure
USE = a seraphic smile

serendipity = making fortunate discoveries
USE = I attribute my success to serendipity

servile = slavish, obedient
USE = servile attitude

simian = monkey like
USE = lemurs have many simian characteristics though they are less intelligent than monkeys

simper = smile foolishly, smirk
USE = She gave her teacher a simpering smile

sinecure = well paid position with little responsibility
USE = my job is no sinecure; I work long hours and have much responsibility

skulk = sneak about
USE = I saw someone skulking in the bushes

slake = to calm down or moderate
USE = I don't think he will ever manage to slake his lust for power

sloth = laziness
USE = the government's sloth in tackling environmental problems

slovenly = sloppy
USE = a slovenly appearance

sobriety = composed
USE = the priest sitting at our table instilled a little sobriety into the occasion

sobriquet = nickname
USE = earned someone the sobriquet

sodden = soaked
USE = Her thin coat quickly became sodden

sojourn = trip, visit
USE = My sojourn in the youth hostel was thankfully short

solace = consolation
USE = Music was a great solace to me during this period

solecism = ungrammatical construction
USE = a grammatical solecism

solicitous = considerate, concerned
USE = a solicitous enquiry after her health

soliloquy = A monologue
USE = *

solstice = furthest point
USE = the winter solstice

somber (BRITISH = sombre) = Gloomy
USE = a somber atmosphere

somnambulist = sleepwalker
USE = *

somnolent = Sleepy
USE = a somnolent summer's afternoon

soporific = sleep inducing
USE = the soporific effect of music

sordid = foul, ignoble, dirty and unpleasant
USE = There are lots of really sordid apartments in the city's poorer areas

spawn = produce
USE = The economic freedom spawned hundreds of new businesses

specious = false but plausible
USE = a specious argument

sporadic = occurring irregularly
USE = sporadic gunfire

sportive = playful
USE = he has a sportive attitude

spurn = reject
USE = She spurned his offers of help

squalid = filthy
USE = Many prisons, even today, are overcrowded and squalid places

staid = demure, sedate, boring
USE = In an attempt to change its staid image, the newspaper has created a new section aimed at younger readers

steadfast = loyal, immovable
USE = steadfast loyalty

stentorian = extremely loud
USE = a stentorian preacher

stigma = mark of disgrace
USE = There is no longer any stigma to being divorced

stilted = formal, stiff, unnatural
USE = He writes in a formal and rather stilted style

stoic = indifferent to pain or pleasure
USE = she must be in pain, despite her stoic attitude

stolid = impassive
USE = He's a very stolid, serious man.

stratagem = trick
USE = He was a master of stratagem.

stricture = negative criticism
USE = The strictures of the United Nations

stultify = inhibit, enfeeble
USE = She felt the repetitive exercises stultified her musical technique so she stopped doing them

stymie = hinder, thwart
USE = we were stymied by the absence of

suave = smooth
USE = He's very suave and sophisticated

sublimate = to repress impulses
USE = to be sublimated into sporting activities

sublime = lofty, excellent
USE = sublime beauty

subterfuge = cunning, ruse
USE = It was clear that they must have obtained the information by subterfuge

succulent = juicy, delicious
USE = a succulent mango

sully = stain
USE = No speck of dirt had ever sullied his hands

supercilious = arrogant
USE = He spoke in a haughty, supercilious voice

supplant = replace
USE = In most offices, the typewriter has been supplanted by the computer

surly = rude, crass
USE = a very surly waiter

surmise = to guess
USE = The police surmise that the robbers have fled the country

surmount = overcome
USE = They managed to surmount all opposition

surreptitious = secretive
USE = During the meeting, I couldn't help noticing her surreptitious glances at the clock

sustenance = supplying the necessities of life
USE = A carrot does not provide much sustenance

swarthy = dark (as in complexion)
USE = a swarthy face

Sybarite = pleasure-seeker, lover of luxury
USE = rich people are not always sybarites

sycophant = flatterer, flunky
USE = The Prime Minister is surrounded by sycophants

taciturn = who does not talk much
USE = He's a reserved, taciturn person

talon = claw of an animal
USE = the hawk's talons

tantamount = equivalent
USE = His refusal to answer was tantamount to an admission of guilt

tawdry = gaudy, cheap
USE = he won a few tawdry trinkets at the village fair

temerity = boldness
USE = She had the temerity to call me a liar

CD 6

ample = enough, spacious, abundant
USE = there is ample space for all

amplify = enlarge, increase, intensify
USE = amplify emotions

ancillary = supplementary, subsidiary, subordinate
USE = ancillary unit

anomaly = deviation from the rule, irregularity
USE = the decision was an anomaly

artifact (BRITISH = artefact) = an object made by human, of historical interest
USE = artifacts in the museum

artisan = a skilled handicraftsman
USE = *

authoritarian = dictator, extremely strict, bossy
USE = authoritarian leader

autocrat = dictator or a high ranking government officer
USE = *

bifurcated = divided into two branches, forked
USE = bifurcated road

blatant = glaring, obvious, showy
USE = blatant lies

bountiful = abundant, plentiful
USE = bountiful crops

brazen = bold, shameless, impudent
USE = a brazen cheat

breach = breaking of a rule, agreement, or law
USE = breach of trust

caricature = cartoon, exaggerated portrait
USE = the overblown caricatures

carnivorous = meat-eating
USE = *

catalyst = something that causes change without being changed
USE = a catalyst for change

centripetal = tending toward the center
USE = centripetal force

chaotic = in utter disorder
USE = a chaotic situation

chauvinist = a man who thinks men are better than women
USE = male chauvinist

complement = To make complete, perfect
USE = The music complements her voice perfectly

composure = Calmness of appearance
USE = lose my composure

compress = to reduce, squeeze
USE = compressed air

constituent = electorate, component, part
USE = The minister worked hard, always talking to his constituents and hearing their problems

constraint = something that limits what you can do
USE = financial constraints

correlation = mutual relationship, association
USE = There's a high correlation between smoking and lung cancer

corrugate = to wrinkle or draw into folds
USE = corrugated box

depose = testify, to remove from a high position
USE = was deposed as a leader

depreciate = To lessen the worth of
USE = our house has depreciated in value

determinate = Definitely limited or fixed, conclusive
USE = the function took place in a determinate order

dexterous = skillful, adroit
USE = a dexterous movement

dwindle = To diminish or become less
USE = dwindled to a tenth of its former size

earthy = crude
USE = she has an earthy sense of humor

entity = being, existence
USE = separate legal entities

equity = impartiality, justice
USE = based on equity and social justice

equivocal = Ambiguous, open to two interpretations
USE = deliberately equivocal

eulogy = high praise
USE = The song was a eulogy to the joys of traveling

exotic = Foreign, romantic
USE = exotic flowers

extemporaneous = unrehearsed
USE = an extemporaneous speech

fabricate = construct
USE = he fabricated an excuse to avoid trouble

fallible = Capable of erring
USE = We place our trust in doctors, but even they are fallible

felicitous = very appropriate, pertinent
USE = He summed up the achievements in one or two felicitous phrases

flair = a natural aptitude
USE = He has a flair for languages

flaunt = to show off
USE = He's got a lot of money but he doesn't flaunt it

flora = plants
USE = flora and fauna

fraudulent = Counterfeit
USE = fraudulent claims

fusion = union, coalition
USE = nuclear fusion

germinate = To begin to develop into an embryo or higher form
USE = The beans will only germinate if the temperature is warm enough

heterogeneous = composed of unlike parts, different
USE = heterogeneous groupings

hypothetical = theoretical, speculative
USE = a hypothetical example

immune = Exempt, as from disease
USE = He seems to be immune to colds

imprudent = unwise
USE = imprudent decision

inception = The beginning
USE = since its inception

inconsequential = Valueless
USE = an inconsequential matter

indefatigable = never getting tired
USE = an indefatigable campaigner

indicative = suggestive, implying
USE = Resumption of the talks is indicative of an improving relationship between the countries

indisputable = not disputed, unquestioned
USE = One fact is indisputable

infantile = childish, immature
USE = infantile behavior

ingenuous = naïve and unsophisticated
USE = it was rather ingenuous of him to ask a complete stranger to look after his luggage

injurious = harmful
USE = cigarette smoking is injurious to your health

innovate = to invent, modernize
USE = always desperate to innovate

integrity = decency, honest, wholeness
USE = a man of the highest integrity

intermittent = starting and stopping
USE = intermittent rain

introspective = looking within oneself
USE = introspective songs

introvert = To turn within
USE = an introverted child

invoke = request assistance or protection
USE = to invoke ancient gods

iota = A small mark or part
USE = I haven't seen one iota of evidence

irreverent = disrespectful
USE = an irreverent comment

jaundice = disease of yellowish discoloration of skin
USE = *

lackluster (BRITISH = lacklustre) = dull, dreary, colorless
USE = a disappointingly lackluster performance

laudable = Praiseworthy
USE = a laudable aim

lexicon = A dictionary
USE = I cannot find this word in any lexicon

litigation = lawsuit
USE = let us settle this amicably rather than going for litigation

lunar = related to the moon
USE = the lunar surface

luscious = Rich, sweet, and delicious
USE = a luscious mango

metaphor = figure of speech comparing two different things
USE = *

microcosm = The world on a small scale
USE = a microcosm of the society

migratory = Wandering from place to place with the seasons
USE = migratory birds

mishap = Misfortune
USE = The parade was very well organized and passed without mishap

mnemonic = related to memory
USE = *

monotony = A lack of variation
USE = with nothing to break the monotony

omnivorous = eating everything
USE = Pigs are omnivorous animals

opportunist = One who takes advantage of circumstances
USE = a ruthless opportunist

orifice = a small opening
USE = The driver was bleeding from every orifice

overt = open to view
USE = overt criticism

paradox = seemingly in contradiction
USE = a curious paradox

parasite = one who lives at another's expense
USE = Financial speculators are parasites upon the national economy

patent = the right to make or sell a new invention
USE = a patent application

pediatrician (BRITISH = paediatrician) = a child doctor
USE = when my child had fever, we took him to a pediatrician

perusal = reading carefully
USE = for their perusal

plenitude = Abundance
USE = we admired the plenitude of rose flowers in the garden

polyglot = Speaking several tongues
USE = a polyglot, he spoke 4 languages

propagate = To spread
USE = Such lies are propagated in the media

reactionary = related to, or favoring reaction
USE = Reactionaries are preventing reforms

reciprocate = To give and take mutually
USE = We invited them to dinner and a week later they reciprocated

regimen = government rule, systematic plan
USE = the doctor put him on a strict regimen

rehabilitate = To restore to a former status
USE = try to rehabilitate prisoners

reminiscence = remembrance of past events
USE = her reminiscences of her experiences are fascinating

renegade = rebel, dissident
USE = A band of renegades had captured the prince

resilient = the quality of springing back
USE = This rubber ball is very resilient

retroactive = applying to an earlier time
USE = to have retroactive effect

sensual = related to the physical senses
USE = sensual pleasure

strident = rough, harsh, caustic, loud
USE = People are put off by his strident voice

subliminal = subconscious, imperceptible
USE = subliminal message

superannuated = retired
USE = the superannuated man still wanted to work

superficial = shallow and phony
USE = at a very superficial level

supple = Easily bent
USE = made of very supple leather

synchronous = happening at the same time
USE = there are many examples of scientists in different parts of the world making synchronous discoveries

tainted = contaminated, corrupt
USE = His reputation was permanently tainted by the financial scandal

talisman = an object supposed to bring good luck
USE = wear the talisman to ward off the evil

theocracy = government by the priests
USE = some religious fans would like theocracy

therapeutic = medicinal
USE = I find gardening very therapeutic

tortuous = with bends or turns
USE = a tortuous route

transcend = To surpass
USE = love transcends everything else

transmute = To change in nature or form
USE = transmute lead into gold

tribute = a gift or statement showing respect
USE = Tributes have been pouring in from all over the world

turbulence = violent agitation
USE = political and cultural turbulence

unobtrusive = inconspicuous, not blatant
USE = unobtrusive and natural-looking

vent = small opening, outlet
USE = a vent in the room

verisimilitude = appearance of being true
USE = lend verisimilitude to the story

versatile = adaptable, all-purpose
USE = a versatile actor

vicarious = substitute, surrogate
USE = a vicarious thrill

viscous = sticky, gluey, thick
USE = melted tar is a viscous substance

warranty = guarantee of a product's soundness
USE = one year warranty

wax = increase, grow
USE = When the moon waxes, it gradually appears larger and rounder each day

weather = endure the effects of weather or other forces
USE = As a small new company they did well to weather the recession

yoke = join together, unite
USE = I don't want to be yoked to him in marriage, said the daughter to her father

temporal = limited by time, secular, not lasting forever
USE = temporal rulers behave as if ruling is their divine right

tenacious = persistent
USE = There has been tenacious local opposition to the new airport

tendentious = biased
USE = tendentious editorials

tenet = doctrine, principle
USE = a tenet of contemporary psychology

tensile = capable of being stretched
USE = tensile strength of a rope

tenuous = thin, insubstantial
USE = a tenuous connection

tepid = lukewarm
USE = a tepid response

terse = concise, brief
USE = Are you feeling any better? "No, " was the terse reply

tether = tie down, tie with a rope
USE = we tethered the horses before we went to sleep

thrall = slave
USE = the captured soldier was held in thrall by the conquering army

thwart = to block or prevent from happening
USE = my plans have been thwarted by the strike

timorous = fearful, timid
USE = his timorous manner betrayed the fear he felt at the moment

tirade = scolding speech
USE = a furious tirade

toady = fawner, sycophant
USE = She was always toadying to the boss

torpid = lethargic, inactive
USE = became torpid before losing consciousness

transient = fleeting, temporary
USE = The city has a large transient population

translucent = clear, lucid, almost transparent
USE = translucent plastic

travesty = caricature, farce, parody
USE = a travesty of justice

trenchant = incisive, penetrating
USE = trenchant criticism

trepidation = fear
USE = with some trepidation

trite = commonplace, insincere
USE = I know it will sound trite, but I've loved being part of this club

truculent = fierce, savage, tending to argue a lot
USE = a truculent teenager

truism = self-evident truth
USE = As far as health is concerned, it's a truism that prevention is better than cure

tryst = meeting, rendezvous
USE = the lovers kept their tryst even though they realized the danger

tumult = commotion
USE = The financial markets are in a tumult

turbid = muddy, clouded
USE = turbid shallow waters

turgid = Swollen, not flowing
USE = a turgid river

turpitude = Depravity, evil
USE = crimes of moral turpitude

tyro = beginner
USE = I look forward to seeing this young tyro's next game

umbrage = resentment
USE = she'll take umbrage if she isn't invited to the party

unctuous = insincere
USE = his unctuous manner

unkempt = messy in appearance
USE = an unkempt lawn

unsullied = spotless
USE = I am happy that my reputation is unsullied

usurp = seize, to appropriate
USE = The powers of local councils were usurped by central government

usury = overcharge, lending money at illegal rates of interest
USE = the loan shark was found guilty of usury

vacillate = To waver
USE = Her mood vacillated between hope and despair

vacuous = inane, empty, not showing intelligence or purpose
USE = a vacuous question

vapid = vacuous, insipid
USE = a vapid television program

venal = willing to do wrong for money
USE = a venal ruler

vendetta = grudge, feud
USE = a personal vendetta

venerable = respected because of age
USE = a venerable tradition

verdant = green, lush
USE = verdant countryside

vex = annoy, to irritate
USE = This issue looks likely to continue to vex the government

vicissitude = changing fortunes
USE = You could say that losing your job is just one of the vicissitudes of life

vie = compete
USE = vying for attention

vignette = scene, decorative design
USE = She wrote several vignettes of small-town life

vilify = defame
USE = vilified by the press

vindicate = free from blame
USE = The investigation vindicated her complaint about the newspaper

virile = manly
USE = the men were young and virile

virulent = deadly, poisonous
USE = a virulent critic

vitiate = spoil, ruin
USE = The Indian military power should never again be vitiated by lack of money

vitriolic = scathing, burning
USE = a vitriolic attack

vociferous = adamant, clamoring
USE = A vociferous opponent

volition = free will
USE = his own volition

voluminous = bulky, extensive, or great quantity
USE = a voluminous account of his life

wallow = indulge, luxuriate
USE = a hippopotamus wallowing in mud

wan = sickly pale
USE = he was pale and wan

wane = dissipate, wither
USE = the popularity was beginning to wane

wary = guarded, careful
USE = wary of giving people my address

welter = confusion, hodgepodge
USE = the company's welter of projects

whet = stimulate, to sharpen
USE = He whetted his knife against the stone

wily = shrewd, clever
USE = a wily politician

winsome = charming
USE = a winsome girl

wizened = shriveled
<u>USE</u> = a wizened old man with yellow skin and deep wrinkles

wraith = ghost
<u>USE</u> = wraith of a voice

wry = twisted, amusing
<u>USE</u> = a wry smile

zephyr = gentle breeze, west wind
<u>USE</u> = when these zephyrs blow, we enjoy sailing

CD 7

amphibian = creature that lives on land and water
USE = frog is an amphibian

anachronism = Anything occurring or existing out of its proper time
USE = For some people, marriage is an anachronism from the days when women needed to be protected

angular = Sharp-cornered or sharp angled
USE = an angular face

anthropomorphous = Nonhuman having or resembling human form or quality
USE = *

apothegm = a short saying
USE = *

appraise = assess, evaluate the value
USE = to appraise the situation

arable = suitable for cultivation
USE = arable farming

asperity = roughness of temper
USE = the asperity of her manner

assay = to analyze or estimate
USE = when they assayed the ore, they found a rich vein

audit = formal examination of final records
USE = an audit team

augury = prophecy or prediction of events
USE = These sales figures are a good augury for another profitable year

aver = to declare to be true
USE = The lawyer averred her client's innocence

aversion = intense dislike
USE = an aversion to something

aviary = cage where birds are kept
USE = the zoo had an aviary

banter = to tease playfully and in good humor
USE = engaging in banter

beatific = supremely happy, angelic, saintly
USE = beatific smile on the child's face

benighted = un enlightened
USE = benighted savages

benison = Blessing
USE = let us pray for the benison of peace on the earth

blanch = bleach, whiten, to take the color out
USE = age had blanched his hair

bludgeon = to hit someone several times with a heavy object
USE = She was bludgeoned to death with a hammer

bolster = To support or make something strong
USE = Strong sales and high profits are bolstering the economy

burnish = To make brilliant or shining
USE = The company is currently trying to burnish its socially responsible image

canny = clever and able to think quickly, especially about money or business
USE = a canny businessman

carnal = of the flesh, sensual
USE = carnal desire

carp = to find faults, complain constantly
USE = to carp about

cavalcade = a procession or sequence
USE = *

celerity = quick moving or acting
USE = *

cession = Surrender, as of possessions or rights
USE = the cession of Alaska to USA

champ = to chew noisily
USE = we were amused by the way he champed his food

chastise = to criticize or punish someone
USE = they chastised the Government for not doing enough

chattel = piece of personal property
USE = goods and chattels

churlish = rude, ungracious
USE = I thought it would be churlish to refuse

circumscribe = To confine within bounds
USE = There followed a series of tightly circumscribed visits to military installations

clairvoyant = who can see the future, having ESP
USE = She went to see a clairvoyant

collate = to sort or put in proper order
USE = to collate data

complaisant = Agreeable, friendly
USE = they obeyed the king's order in a complaisant manner

consequential = important, as a result
USE = Certain consequential changes of the existing text

contumacious = rebellious
USE = the contumacious mob

cuisine = cookery, style of cooking
USE = French cuisine

culmination = climax, final stage
USE = the culmination of years of practice and hard work

curator = in charge of a library or museum
USE = *

daunt = to frighten, subdue
USE = She was not at all daunted by the size of the problem

declivity = a place that declines or slopes downwards
USE = the children loved to ski down the declivity

deranged = insane, delirious, maniacal
USE = a deranged criminal

derivative = copied or adapted, not original
USE = His painting is terribly derivative

descry = To discern, to discover or reveal
USE = in the distance, we could barely descry the enemy vessels

diffidence = shyness, lack of confidence
USE = you must overcome your diffidence if you want to become a salesman

dirge = lament with music, funeral hymn
USE = the funeral dirge stirred us to tears

discomfit = To put to confusion, discomfort
USE = the trick will discomfit the enemy

discordant = harsh-sounding, badly out of tune
USE = struck a slightly discordant note

dissimulate = to disguise
USE = she tried to dissimulate her grief by her exuberant attitude

distaff = the female branch of a family
USE = his ancestors on the distaff side were as famous as on his father's side

dolt = a stupid person
USE = a pack of dolts and idiots

domineer = to rule over something in a tyrannical way
USE = the best teachers are those who guide and not domineer

doughty = brave, dauntless
USE = a doughty campaigner

dross = waste matter, worthless impurities
USE = So much of what's on TV is pure dross

dyspeptic = suffering from indigestion, gloomy and irritable
USE = eating too much made him feel dyspeptic

effluvium = noxious smells
USE = the effluvium and poisons in the air

effusive = expressing emotion without restraint
USE = an effusive welcome

elation = exhilaration, joy
USE = a sense of elation

eloquence = fluent and effective speech
USE = renowned for her eloquence and beauty

emollient = cream for softening, making supple
USE = he applied an emollient on the inflamed area

ensconce = to hide safely, settle comfortably
USE = After dinner, I ensconced myself in a deep armchair with a book

enunciate = verbalize, articulate
USE = He doesn't enunciate very clearly

epilogue = The close of a narrative or poem
USE = many did not remain to hear the epilogue

epitome = A simplified representation
USE = she is the epitome of Indian elegance

equestrian = one who rides on horseback
USE = equestrian events

excoriate = to denounce
USE = excoriating reviews

exculpate = to clear of blame or fault
USE = The pilot of the aircraft will surely be exculpated when all the facts are known

expatiate = to discuss in detail, elaborate
USE = She expatiated on her work

expatriate = who does not live in one's own country
USE = A large community of expatriates

expurgate = to purify by removing obscenities
USE = The book was expurgated to make it suitable for children

extrinsic = not inherent or essential, coming from without
USE = do not be fooled by extrinsic causes

extrovert = an outgoing person
USE = extrovert vs. introvert

fell = to chop, cut down
USE = A great number of trees were felled

fervid = fervent, passionate
USE = his fervid hope

fetter = to restrain, to bind
USE = He felt fettered by a nine-to-five office existence

finicky = meticulous, fussy
USE = He's terribly finicky about his food

fissure = a crack or break
USE = the mountain climber secured footholds in tiny fissures in the rock

flaccid = limp, flabby, weak
USE = lackluster and flaccid

flamboyant = Characterized by extravagance
USE = a flamboyant gesture

fluster = confuse
USE = the sudden question flustered the student

forbearance = Patient endurance or toleration of offenses
USE = He thanked his employees for the forbearance they had shown during the company's difficult times

forte = A strong point
USE = I'm afraid sewing isn't one of my fortes

fractious = wayward, unruly, disorderly
USE = a fractious child

frenzied = feverishly fast, hectic
USE = a scene of frenzied activity

funereal = mournful, appropriate to a funeral
USE = funereal music

gall = bitterness, nerve
USE = has the gall to ask them for money

gambol = Playful leaping or frisking
USE = Lambs were gamboling around in the spring sunshine

gaunt = thin, emaciated
USE = Her face was gaunt and gray

gustatory = relevant to the sense of tasting
USE = gustatory pleasures

hallow = to make holy
USE = she was laid to rest in hallowed ground

hoary = white, old
USE = a few hoary old jokes

holocaust = widespread destruction
USE = A nuclear holocaust

ignominious = Shameful
USE = an ignominious defeat

impious = not devout in religion
USE = impious remarks

implacable = unappeasable, merciless
USE = an implacable enemy

improvident = lacking foresight or thrift
USE = to mend his improvident ways

incarnadine = blood-red in color
USE = *

indenture = bound to another by contract
USE = He was indentured to a carpenter

interstice = a small space between things
USE = plants were growing in the interstices
between the bricks

iridescent = showing many colors
USE = iridescent materials

jettison = to throw overboard, abandon
USE = The station has jettisoned educational
broadcasts

jingoism = extremely aggressive and militant
patriotism
USE = Patriotism can turn into jingoism and
intolerance very quickly

lackadaisical = Listless, idle
USE = the service was lackadaisical

languor = Lassitude of body or depression
USE = he had fallen into languor and was
depressed

lapidary = relating to precious stones
USE = she employed a lapidary to cut a large
diamond

latitude = freedom from narrow limitations
USE = you have permitted your son too much
latitude in this matter

lionize = treat as a celebrity
USE = she enjoyed being lionized and adored by
the public

loiter = dawdle, loaf
USE = A gang of youths were loitering outside the
cinema

lull = moment of calm
USE = The motion of the car almost lulled her to
sleep

maritime = Situated on or near the sea
USE = The temperature change in winter is less
pronounced in maritime areas

megalomania = mental state with delusions of
wealth and power
USE = Hitler suffered from megalomania

mendacious = Untrue
USE = Some of these statements are misleading and
some downright mendacious

meretricious = Alluring by false or gaudy show
USE = meretricious and superficial

molt = to shed hair, skin periodically
USE = snakes molt

monastic = related to monks
USE = a monastic life

morbid = abnormally gloomy
USE = a morbid fascination with death

naiveté = a lack of worldly wisdom
USE = He demonstrated a worrying naivete about
political issues

nihilism = a belief in nothing, extreme
skepticism
USE = nihilism holds that existence has no meaning

nomadic = moving from place to place
USE = a nomadic life

non sequitur = an irrelevant conclusion
USE = the student paper was full of non sequiturs

nuptial = relating to marriage
USE = nuptial vows

objurgate = to chide, scold
USE = she will objurgate us publicly for this offense

opalescent = iridescent, displaying colors
USE = the opalescent scales of a fish

ornithologist = scientist who studies birds
USE = *

orotund = pompously said
USE = the politician's orotund voice was an asset

palette = board for mixing paints
USE = students can use a paper palette when they learn painting

pastiche = imitation of another's style
USE = The film is a skilful, witty pastiche of "Jaws"

patricide = murder of one's own father
USE = *

peculation = theft of money or goods
USE = the auditors discovered her peculations

pediment = triangular gable on a roof or façade
USE = the pediment of the building was filled with sculptures

penumbra = partial shadow in an eclipse
USE = *

permeable = penetrable
USE = permeable membrane

philology = study of words
USE = *

plaintiff = injured person in a lawsuit
USE = *

plangent = plaintive, resounding sadly
USE = the plangent tones of the singers

politic = expedient, prudent, well devised
USE = It would not be politic for you to be seen there

potable = suitable for drinking
USE = potable water

presentiment = sense of foreboding
USE = a presentiment of what might lie ahead

primordial = existing at the beginning, rudimentary
USE = primordial soup

pummel = beat, attack
USE = They were pummeled in the second round

putrid = dirty, rotten
USE = putrid smell

quintessence = The most essential part of anything
USE = *

ramshackle = dilapidated, falling to pieces
USE = a ramshackle old shed

ratiocination = reasoning
USE = the author's use of ratiocination

raucous = Harsh sounding
USE = Raucous laughter came from the next room

ravenous = extremely hungry
USE = I'm ravenous - where's the supper

rectitude = moral uprightness
USE = unquestioned moral rectitude

refectory = dining hall
USE = all students could eat at the same time in the huge refectory

remediable = capable of being corrected
USE = let us be grateful that the damage is remediable

remonstrate = to protest or object
USE = to remonstrate against the new rules

retinue = group of attendants
USE = a large retinue of aides and bodyguards

rococo = ornate, highly decorated
USE = the rococo style in furniture

roil = to disturb or cause disorder
USE = be careful when you pour not to roil the wine

salubrious = healthy
USE = salubrious part of town

serenity = calm, peacefulness
USE = I admired her serenity in the midst of so much chaos

serrated = toothed, with a zigzag edge
USE = a knife with a serrated edge

sinuous = Curving in and out
USE = the sinuous path through the trees

slough = to discard or shed
USE = Snakes slough their skin regularly

sluggard = lazy, inactive person
USE = "you are a sluggard", shouted the angry father to his son

sophist = person good at arguing deviously
USE = a sophist would argue

sophomoric = immature and overconfident
USE = a sophomoric sense of humor

staccato = marked by abrupt, clear-cut sounds
USE = The music suddenly changed from a smooth melody to a staccato rhythm

succinct = Concise
USE = Keep your letter succinct and to the point

synthetic = artificial, imitation
USE = synthetic fibers

threnody = a sad poem or song, dirge
USE = many poets wrote threnodies about him when he died

tremulous = trembling, fearful
USE = her tremulous hand

tundra = treeless plain found in Arctic or sub arctic regions
USE = Few plants grow in tundra regions

upbraid = to scold sharply
USE = she consistently upbraided those in authority

vagrant = An idle wanderer
USE = shelters and food for vagrants

variegated = many-colored
USE = a variegated plant

vaunted = boasted, bragged
USE = the vaunted new scheme has been shown to have serious weaknesses

veracious = truthful, accurate
USE = veracious and reliable

verity = Truth
USE = in a search for eternal verities

vernal = related to spring
USE = vernal showers

wrangle = loud quarrel
USE = a lengthy wrangle about costs

CD 8

abbreviate = shorten
USE = Reader's Digest prints abbreviated articles

abolish = annul
USE = abolish the old law

aboriginal = indigenous
USE = aboriginal people

abridge = to condense, shorten
USE = Abridged version of a book<u>hint</u>

abscond = to run away secretly
USE = the accused was absconding

abstract = theoretical, intangible, complex, difficult
USE = it is too abstract for me to understand

accessory = attachment, ornament; accomplice, partner
USE = bathroom accessories or an accessory to murder<u>hint</u>

accomplice = one who aids a lawbreaker
USE = the accomplice was also sentenced to jail

accord = to reconcile, come to an agreement
USE = a peace accord

accrue = to accumulate, grow by additions
USE = accrue vacations

acoustic = pertaining to sound
USE = an acoustic guitar

adage = proverb, old saying
USE = an old adage

adapt = adjust to changing conditions, accommodate
USE = India is adapting well to the computer age

adept = skillful
USE = She's very adept at dealing with the media

adhere = stick to or to follow without deviation
USE = adhere strictly to guidelines<u>hint</u>

adulterate = contaminate, corrupt, make impure
USE = adulterated food

adverse = unfavorable, unlucky, harmful
USE = adverse reaction to medicine

adversity = hardship
USE = cheerful in adversity

advocate = to speak in favor of
USE = Gandhiji advocated vegetarian food

aesthetic = pleasing to the senses, beautiful, or related to art
USE = aesthetic appeal.

affable = friendly, easy to approach
USE = an affable person

affidavit = sworn written statement
USE = submit affidavit

affiliation = connection
USE = political affiliation

affinity = fondness or similarity
USE = a natural affinity

agenda = plan, timetable
USE = a hidden agenda

aggregate = total, collective mass or sum
USE = I got 90% marks aggregate and 95% in Maths

agitate = stir up
USE = they continued to agitate for social rights

agnostic = not knowing whether God exists
USE = *

agrarian = relating to farming or rural matters
USE = an agrarian society

alias = assumed name
USE = Jawaharlal Nehru, alias, Chacha Nehru

alienate = estrange, antagonize
USE = to alienate someone<u>hint</u>

alleviate = lessen, assuage, relieve, improve partially
USE = take tablets to alleviate pain

allocate = distribute
USE = allocate work to people

aloof = detached, indifferent
USE = he seems arrogant and aloof

altercation = argument, noisy dispute
USE = the altercation ended their friendship

amass = collect
USE = amass enormous wealth

ambiguous = unclear, uncertain; subject to multiple interpretations
USE = an ambiguous statement

ambivalence = conflicting emotions; attitude of uncertainty
USE = ambivalence towards something

amend = correct
USE = to amend a law

amenities = courtesies, comforts
USE = public amenities

amnesty = pardon
USE = under the terms of the amnesty

amoral = without morals
USE = Humans, he argues, are amoral and what guides them is not any sense of morality but an instinct for survival.

analgesic = pain-soother
USE = a mild analgesic

analogy = point by point comparison
USE = he used analogies to make his point clear

animated = exuberant
USE = an animated conversation

annihilate = destroy
USE = a city annihilated by an atom bomb

annotate = to add explanatory notes
USE = the officer annotated the application before forwarding it

anomalous = abnormal
USE = an anomalous artery

antagonistic = hostile
USE = antagonistic towards all critics

ape = mimic
USE = the new building merely apes the classical traditions

apprehensive = anxious
USE = a bit apprehensive about

aptitude = ability
USE = personal aptitudes and abilities

archives = public records
USE = archive film

arrears = in debt
USE = rent arrears

aspirant = contestant
USE = an aspirant to the throne

aspiration = ambition
USE = political aspirations

assimilate = absorb
USE = the refugees have assimilated into the local community

asylum = place of refuge
USE = apply for political asylum

attribute = ascribe
USE = an essential attribute for success

attrition = deterioration, reduction
USE = a costly war of attrition

atypical = abnormal
USE = The sociable behavior of lions is considered atypical of the cat family

audacity = boldness
USE = It took a lot of audacity to stand up and criticize the chairman.

automaton = robot
USE = I do the same route to work every day, like an automaton

avatar = incarnation
USE = Sri Krishna is an avatar

avid = enthusiastic
USE = an avid cricket fan

avocation = hobby
USE = I am a rocket scientist, but music is my avocation

barrister = lawyer
USE = a barrister of law

benediction = divine blessing
USE = his presence was such a benediction

benevolent = kind
USE = a benevolent action

berserk = crazed
USE = go berserk

biennial = occurring every two years
USE = a biennial function

bleak = cheerless
USE = bleak future

bloated = swollen
USE = a bloated stomach

bravado = feigned bravery
USE = his bravado got him in trouble

caliber (BRITISH = calibre) = ability
USE = of high-caliber

camaraderie = fellowship
USE = a tremendous sense of camaraderie

capillary = thin tube
USE = capillary in hands

caption = title
USE = the photo with an interesting caption

carcinogenic = causing cancer
USE = cigarettes are carcinogenic

cartographer = mapmaker
USE = *

celestial = heavenly
USE = The moon is a celestial body

celibate = abstaining from sex
USE = *

cerebral = pertaining to the brain
USE = cerebral films

cessation = a stopping
USE = a smoking cessation program

chronic = continual
USE = a chronic disease

coercion = force
USE = police used coercion

collaborate = work together
USE = they collaborated on the project

comatose = stupor
USE = By midnight I was virtually comatose

commandeer = seize for military use
USE = *

commemorate = observe
USE = a ceremony to commemorate the independence movement

commiserate = empathize
USE = I began by commiserating with her over the defeat

compact = covenant
USE = They made a compact not to reveal any details

compatible = well-matched, harmonious
USE = This software may not be compatible with older operating systems

compendium = summary
USE = the Gardener's Compendium

compensatory = redeeming
USE = compensatory damages

comprehensive = thorough
USE = comprehensive insurance policy

concise = brief
USE = clear and concise

conclusive = convincing, ending doubt
USE = conclusive evidence

concoct = devise
USE = He concocted a story about working late at the office

concurrent = simultaneous
USE = three concurrent prison sentences

confidant = trusted friend
USE = a close confidant

congruence = conformity
USE = he demonstrated congruence of two triangles

contempt = disdain
USE = She's beneath contempt

contiguous = adjacent, abutting
USE = Rajasthan and Gujarat are contiguous states

contraband = illicit goods
USE = *

converge = come together
USE = The paths all converge at the main gate

conversant = familiar
USE = I'm conversant with the topic

converse = opposite
USE = a converse opinion

conviction = strongly held belief
USE = a lifelong conviction

cordial = friendly
USE = a cordial smile

coup = master stroke
USE = a tremendous coup for the local paper

credulity = gullibility
USE = the witch doctor took advantage of the natives' credulity

crux = gist, key
USE = the crux of the problem

culinary = pertaining to cooking
USE = culinary equipment

cumbersome = unwieldy
USE = cumbersome equipment

cynical = scornful of the motives of others
USE = many people have become cynical about politicians

dais = platform
USE = speaking from the dais

debacle = a rout, defeat
USE = The collapse of the company was described as the greatest financial debacle in the history

decimate = destroy
USE = populations of endangered animals have been decimated

decipher = decode
USE = to decipher someone's handwriting

defeatist = one who is resigned to defeat
USE = a defeatist attitude

delete = remove
USE = deleted from the article

deliberate = ponder
USE = deliberated the question at great length

delineate = draw a line around, describe
USE = The boundary was clearly delineated

delude = deceive
USE = don't delude yourself

derogatory = degrading
USE = derogatory comment

despicable = contemptible
USE = a despicable crime

despise = loathe
USE = He despised himself for being such a coward

deterrent = hindrance
USE = a nuclear deterrent

devotee = enthusiast, follower
USE = devotees of cricket

dilemma = difficult choice
USE = dilemma about whether or not to go

dire = dreadful
USE = dire consequences

discernible = visible
USE = discernible difference between things

discerning = observant
USE = a discerning customer

disgruntle = disappointed
USE = the passengers were disgruntled by the delay

disinclination = unwillingness
USE = disinclination to do any work

dismantle = take apart
USE = She dismantled the washing machine

dissertation = lecture
USE = Ph D dissertation

distortion = misinterpret, lie
USE = a gross distortion of the facts

diva = prima donna
USE = a pop diva

diversion = pastime
USE = watching TV is a diversion from studies

diversity = variety
USE = unity in diversity

divulge = disclose
USE = he would not divulge how much the pen cost.

document = verify
USE = legal documents

domicile = home
USE = domicile certificate

dubious = Doubtful
USE = dubious means

dynamic = energetic
USE = young and dynamic

eccentric = odd, weird
USE = an eccentric professor

effeminate = unmanly
USE = An effeminate man entered the room

effervescence = exuberance
USE = her natural effervescence made her look happy

efficacy = effectiveness
USE = efficacy of a drug

elaboration = detailed explanation
USE = This point needs greater elaboration

elusive = evasive
USE = Success, however, remained elusive for her

embezzlement = theft
USE = embezzlement of company funds

encompass = contain, encircle
USE = the new music tape encompasses a wide range of music

encroach = trespass
USE = drive to remove encroachments

endear = enamor
USE = She is unlikely to endear herself to her colleagues with such an aggressive approach

endorse = approve
USE = expected to endorse these recommendations

enhance = improve
USE = plants enhance the beauty of any place

ensue = follow immediately
USE = The police officer said that he had placed the man under arrest and that a scuffle had ensued

entomology = the study of insects
USE = professor of entomology

entrepreneur = businessman
USE = he left the job to become an entrepreneur

equable = even-tempered
USE = an equable climate

esteem = respect
USE = held in high esteem

evasive = elusive
USE = evasive replies

execute = put into effect
USE = execute a will

exodus = departure, migration
USE = exodus of people from villages to cities

expedite = hasten
USE = expedite reply

expertise = knowledge, ability
USE = expertise in law

exploit = utilize, milk
USE = exploit our natural resources

faction = clique, sect
USE = the left-wing faction of the party

falter = waver
USE = the conversation faltered for a moment

fanfare = publicity
USE = there was much fanfare

fauna = animals
USE = flora and fauna

fictitious = invented, imaginary
USE = a fictitious story

figment = falsehood, fantasy
USE = a figment of my imagination

finale = conclusion
USE = a grand finale

foresight = ability to predict the future
USE = she had the foresight to buy a house before the prices rose

futile = hopeless
USE = futile effort

gambit = plot
USE = a clever opening gambit

generic = general
USE = generic drugs

germane = Relevant
USE = a germane answer

gist = essence
USE = That was the gist of what he said

glut = surplus, excess
USE = cause a glut in the market

glutton = one who eats too much
USE = be a gourmet without being a glutton

gravity = seriousness
USE = the gravity of the situation

grudging = reluctant
USE = the grudging respect of her boss

hallucination = delusion
USE = auditory hallucinations

harass = torment
USE = stop harassing me

herbivorous = feeding on plants
USE = a herbivorous dinosaur

hirsute = bearded
USE = a hirsute individual with a heavy black beard

hue = color
USE = there are fish of every hue

humility = humbleness
USE = He doesn't have the humility to admit when he's wrong

husbandry = management
USE = animal husbandry

hybrid = crossbreed
USE = hybrid flower or hybrid seed

hydrophobia = fear of water
USE = *

imbibe = drink
USE = the dry soil imbibed the rains quickly

imminent = about to happen
USE = imminent danger

impending = approaching
USE = impending disaster

implement = carry out, execute
USE = The changes will be implemented next year

import = meaning, significance
USE = the visit is of no import

improvise = invent
USE = I hadn't prepared a speech so I suddenly had to improvise

inanimate = inorganic, lifeless
USE = an inanimate object

incentive = stimulus
USE = Tax incentive

incite = foment, provoke
USE = he incited racial hatred

increment = step, increase
USE = salary increments

indemnity = insurance, compensate against loss
USE = city will indemnify all home owners

indifferent = unconcerned
USE = indifferent attitude

indiscriminate = random
USE = an indiscriminate terrorist attack

inebriate = To intoxicate
USE = the inebriated driver

infamous = notorious
USE = infamous criminal<u>hint</u>

inherent = innate, inborn
USE = an inherent distrust of lawyer

inhibit = restrain
USE = This drug inhibits the growth of tumors

intelligentsia = the intellectual elite of society
USE = *

intervene = interfere, mediate
USE = The Central Bank intervened

intimate = allude to
USE = She has intimated that she will resign if she loses the vote

inverse = directly opposite
USE = in inverse proportion to

CD 9

ironic = oddly contrary to what is expected
USE = an ironic comment

irrelevant = unrelated, immaterial
USE = irrelevant to the present investigation

irreparable = cannot be repaired
USE = irreparable damage

junta = small ruling group
USE = military junta

juxtapose = to place side by side
USE = The exhibition juxtaposes Picasso's early drawings with some of his later works

kaleidoscope = series of changing events
USE = a kaleidoscope of colors

kindred = similar
USE = kindred spirit

kleptomania = impulse to steal
USE = he used to steal as he was suffering from kleptomania

languish = weaken
USE = After languishing in obscurity for many years

laudatory = commendable
USE = the laudatory comments by the critics

legacy = A bequest
USE = The war left a legacy of hatred

lethargic = drowsy, sluggish
USE = feeling tired and lethargic

liaison = relationship, affair
USE = a liaison officer

Lilliputian = very small
USE = the model was built on a Lilliputian scale

liquidate = eliminate
USE = he was able to liquidate his debts

loath = reluctant
USE = I'm loath to

lucrative = profitable
USE = lucrative business

luster (BRITISH = lustre) = gloss
USE = the rich luster of well-polished furniture

Machiavellian = politically crafty, cunning
USE = a Machiavellian plan

malaise = uneasiness, weariness
USE = the current economic malaise

malign = defame
USE = a malign influence

malignant = virulent, pernicious
USE = malignant cancer cells

mammoth = huge
USE = a mammoth task

mandate = A command
USE = seeking a fresh mandate

manifesto = proclamation
USE = election manifesto

maternal = motherly
USE = maternal uncle

matrix = mold or die, array
USE = the cast around the matrix was cracked

mediocre = average
USE = a mediocre school

memento = A souvenir
USE = a memento of our holiday

mercantile = commercial
USE = mercantile system of accounting

meteoric = swift
USE = a meteoric rise to fame

methodical = systematic, careful
USE = a very methodical person

milieu = environment
USE = the social and cultural milieu

militant = combative
USE = a militant group

mirage = illusion
USE = For her, victory was just a distant mirage

mogul = powerful person
USE = industry moguls

moratorium = postponement
USE = a moratorium on nuclear weapons testing

motif = theme
USE = a flower motif

mutilate = maim
USE = the body had been mutilated beyond recognition

narcissism = self-love
USE = seem to suffer from narcissism

nepotism = favoritism
USE = guilty of nepotism and corruption

nexus = link
USE = there is no nexus between these two events

nirvana = bliss
USE = Buddha achieved nirvana

notorious = wicked, widely known
USE = a notorious criminal

novel = new, unique
USE = a novel idea

nurture = nourish, foster
USE = a carefully nurtured garden

obese = fat
USE = doctors advise the obese people to lose weight

objective = unbiased, goal
USE = my objective is to help you

obligatory = required
USE = The medical examination was obligatory

obtrusive = forward, meddlesome
USE = The logo was still visible but less obtrusive in light blue

Occident = the West
USE = *

occult = mystical
USE = occult powers

odyssey = journey
USE = a film about one man's odyssey

oligarchy = aristocracy
USE = *

onslaught = attack
USE = the forces could withstand an enemy onslaught

opiate = narcotic, sleep producer, pain reducer
USE = *

optional = elective
USE = optional subjects

ordinance = law
USE = a city ordinance

orient = align
USE = to orient yourself

ornate = lavishly decorated
USE = an ornate ceiling and gold mirrors

ornithology = study of birds
USE = *

orthodox = conventional
USE = orthodox medicine

ostracize = ban
USE = His colleagues ostracized him

pachyderm = thick skinned animal, elephant
USE = *

painstaking = taking great care
USE = painstaking research

parable = allegory
USE = the wise man told parables

parameter = limit
USE = keep within the parameters

paraphernalia = equipment
USE = cricket paraphernalia

parlance = local speech
USE = in common parlance

partial = incomplete
USE = partial withdrawal of troops

partiality = bias
USE = there was no evidence of partiality in the selection process

pathetic = pitiful
USE = a pathetic sight

peon = common worker
USE = an office peon

periphery = outer boundary
USE = the periphery of the city center

permeate = spread throughout
USE = permeated every section of society

perpetrate = commit
USE = to perpetrate atrocities against innocent people

perquisite = reward, bonus
USE = On getting promoted, he got a car as a perquisite

personable = charming
USE = he is personable

pervade = permeate
USE = The film is a reflection of the violence that pervades the society

philanthropist = altruist
USE = a wealthy philanthropist

plagiarize = pirate, counterfeit
USE = The book contains numerous plagiarized passages

plenary = full
USE = a plenary session

polygamist = one who has many wives
USE = *

posthumous = after death
USE = a posthumous award

postulate = supposition, premise
USE = Einstein postulated the theory of relativity

potion = brew
USE = a magic potion

potpourri = medley
USE = a potpourri of arts and media reports

precedent = an act that serves as an example
USE = There are several precedents for

precise = accurate, detailed
USE = precise location

predecessor = one who proceeds
USE = My predecessor worked in this job for twelve years

preempt (BRITISH = pre-empt) = commandeer
USE = in order to pre-empt criticism

prelude = introduction
USE = a prelude to wide-ranging reforms

prestige = reputation, renown
USE = international prestige

prevail = triumph
USE = common sense will prevail in the end

privy = aware of private matters
USE = privy to conversations

probe = examine
USE = The article probes the causes of

promiscuous = sexually indiscreet
USE = promiscuous in his youth

prone = inclined, predisposed
USE = prone to disease

protege = ward, pupil
USE = his young protégé

provoke = incite
USE = was provoked into the argument

pulsate = throb
USE = The whole room was pulsating with music

puny = weak, small
USE = My car only has a puny little engine

qualified = limited
USE = I'd like to qualify my criticisms

queue = line
USE = a queue at the cinema hall

rebuttal = replay, counterargument
USE = She issued a point-by-point rebuttal of the company's accusations

recipient = one who receives
USE = a recipient of the Bharat Ratna award

reciprocal = mutual, return in kind
USE = reciprocal support

reconcile = adjust, balance
USE = It is difficult to reconcile science and religion

recourse = appeal, resort
USE = without recourse to litigation

regime = a government
USE = the former Communist regime

remedial = corrective
USE = remedial classes

repertoire = stock of works
USE = an extensive repertoire

replenish = refill
USE = the supplies were replenished daily

replica = copy
USE = exact replica of the original

reputed = supposed
USE = She is reputed to be 25 years younger than her husband

requisite = Necessary
USE = the requisite skills

reserve = self control
USE = reserved nature

resolution = determination
USE = He showed great resolution in facing the robbers

resonant = reverberating
USE = a deep resonant voice

sadist = one who takes pleasure in hurting others
USE = the school teacher was a sadist

saga = story
USE = an ongoing saga of marriage problems

saline = salty
USE = saline solution

satire = ridicule
USE = political satire

saturate = soak
USE = The grass had been saturated by overnight rain

scapegoat = one who takes blame for others
USE = The captain was made a scapegoat for the team's failure

sensuous = appealing to the senses
USE = the sensuous feel of the silk sheets

severance = division
USE = a severance agreement

sham = pretense
USE = a sham marriage

shambles = disorder
USE = Our economy is in a shambles

shrewd = clever
USE = a shrewd politician

sibling = brother or sister
USE = sibling rivalry

simile = figure of speech
USE = the poem contains a simile

sinister = Evil
USE = sinister-looking man

spectrum = range
USE = The colors of the spectrum

stamina = vigor, endurance
USE = a great test of stamina

subservient = servile, submissive
USE = a subservient role

subsidiary = subordinate
USE = a subsidiary role

superimpose = cover, place on top of
USE = a picture of a dove superimposed on a battle scene

supine = Lying on the back
USE = supine posture

surrogate = substitute
USE = a surrogate child

surveillance = close watch
USE = surveillance cameras.

symmetry = harmony, congruence
USE = a pleasing symmetry

tautological = repetitious
USE = *

terminology = nomenclature
USE = scientific terminology

throttle = choke
USE = Sometimes he annoys me so much that I could throttle him

titillate = arouse
USE = So many adverts nowadays are designed to titillate

transcribe = write a copy
USE = the conversations were transcribed by typists

transgression = trespass, offense
USE = Who is supposed to have committed these transgressions

traverse = cross
USE = he traversed the continent from west to east

treatise = book, dissertation
USE = a six-volume treatise on patent law

trek = journey
USE = trekking through forests

ulterior = hidden, covert
USE = an ulterior motive

ultimatum = demand
USE = He gave her an ultimatum

uncanny = mysterious, inexplicable
USE = an uncanny resemblance

ungainly = awkward
USE = Ducks are ungainly on land

unilateral = action taken by only one party
USE = unilateral nuclear disarmament

unison = together
USE = Try to sing in unison

unmitigated = complete, harsh
USE = an unmitigated disaster

unprecedented = without previous occurrence
USE = environmental destruction on an unprecedented scale

upshot = result
USE = The upshot of the discussions is that

venue = location
USE = The hotel is an ideal venue

vogue = fashion, chic
USE = this style is in vogue

warrant = justification
USE = it did not warrant such severe punishment

CD 10

anecdotes (BRITISH = anecdote) = story, usually funny account of an event
USE = a speech full of anecdotes

ardent = passionate, enthusiastic
USE = ardent believer

arsenal = ammunition store house
USE = The army planned to attack enemy arsenals

artless = naïve, simple, open and honest
USE = an artless businessman

ascend = to rise or climb
USE = They slowly ascended the steep path up the mountain

assert = affirm, attest
USE = He asserts that she stole money from him

asymmetric = uneven, not corresponding in size, shape, position
USE = a trendy asymmetric haircut

bent = natural inclination towards something, determined
USE = She has a scientific bent

bibliography = list of books or sources of information
USE = bibliography at the end of the book

bilateral = Two-sided
USE = bilateral agreement

biped = two-footed animal
USE = *

boon = blessing, something to be thankful for
USE = Guide dogs are a great boon to the partially sighted

bovine = cow-like
USE = a bovine virus

buffet = blow, strike or hit
USE = The little boat was buffeted mercilessly by the waves

buffoon = fool, clown
USE = he looked like a buffoon in the red and green suit

candid = frank, unrehearsed, fair
USE = candid opinion

cardiologist = physician who specializes in the diseases of the heart
USE = if you have a chest pain, see a cardiologist

coagulate = thicken
USE = The sauce coagulated as it cooled down

coffer = strong box, large chest for money
USE = government coffers

cohabit = live together
USE = cohabiting couples

commend = praise, compliment
USE = The judge commended her on her bravery

commission = authorization to perform a task, or fee payable to an agent
USE = Do you take commissions

commute = lessen punishment
USE = the commute takes him 30 minutes

compatriot = fellow countryman
USE = *

compelling = convincing
USE = compel someone to do something

compensate = make up for, to repay or reimburse
USE = Victims of the crash will be compensated for their injuries

composed = cool, self-possessed, acting calm
USE = She finally stopped crying and composed herself

compound = augment, composed of several parts
USE = Salt is a compound of sodium and chlorine

compulsive = obsessive, fanatic
USE = compulsive gambling

concede = yield, grant, admit
USE = the government did not concede to rebel demands

consign = assign, to commit, entrust
USE = they were consigned to a life of poverty

consolation = something providing comfort or solace for a loss or hardship
USE = If it's any consolation to you

consolidate = unite, strengthen, to combine, incorporate
USE = to consolidate a position

constrained = confined, forced, compelled, restrained
USE = The country's progress was constrained by a leader who refused to look forward.

contend = struggle, to battle, clash, compete
USE = three chess players are contending for the prize

cosmopolitan = worldly, sophisticated, free from local prejudices
USE = Mumbai is a cosmopolitan city

credulous = believing, gullible, trusting
USE = *

culprit = offender, guilty person
USE = who is the culprit

cumulative = accumulate
USE = cumulative effect of

decorum = protocol, proper behavior, etiquette
USE = to act with proper decorum

deface = mar, disfigure, vandalize, to mar the appearance of
USE = jailed for defacing the poster of the Presidenthint

defame = slander or disgrace
USE = The opposition party tried to defame the Prime Ministerhint

defer = postpone, to submit or yield
USE = I defer to your judgment.

delegate = authorize, to give powers to another
USE = As a boss you have to delegate

desist = to stop doing something
USE = The high winds are expected to desist tomorrow

deter = discourage, prevent from happening
USE = the security alarm will deter thieves from coming to this park

dilatory = procrastinating, slow, tending to delay
USE = dilatory tactics

dispute = Debate, to quarrel
USE = a bitter dispute

disrepute = disgrace, dishonor
USE = to fall into disrepute

distrust = suspect, disbelief and suspicion
USE = mutual distrust

divine = foretell
USE = a divine intervention

divisive = causing conflict
USE = divisive forces

donor = contributor
USE = a blood donor

editorialize (BRITISH = editorialise) = express an opinion
USE = *

egocentric = self-centered
USE = Babies are entirely egocentric, concerned only with when they will next be fed

empathy = compassion, sympathy, identification with another's feelings
USE = *

entrench = fortify, establish
USE = It's very difficult to change attitudes that have become so deeply entrenched over the years

enumerate = count, list, itemize
USE = enumerate the contents

eradicate = abolish
USE = eradicate poverty

escalate = intensify
USE = His financial problems escalated after he became unemployed

ethical = conforming to accepted standards of behavior, moral
USE = ethical problems

euphoria = elation, feeling of well-being or happiness
USE = in a state of euphoria

evade = to avoid
USE = don't evade taxes

excerpt = selection from a book, extract
USE = excerpt of a new book

excommunicate = to bar from membership in the church
USE = *

excruciate = torture, agonize
USE = excruciating pain

expansive = sweeping
USE = an expansive view from the window

extrapolate = infer, to estimate
USE = extrapolate a trend from a small sample

extremity = farthest point
USE = The wood lies on the southern extremity of the city

facility = skill, aptitude, ease in doing something
USE = His facility for languages is astounding

fluctuate = waver, vary
USE = Vegetable prices fluctuate according to the season

foreclose = exclude
USE = it foreclosed any chance of diplomatic compromise

forgo = relinquish, to go without
USE = She had to forgo her early desire to be a writer

forsake = abandon
USE = Do not forsake me!

founder = sink
USE = The boat foundered in a heavy storm, taking many of the passengers with it

geriatrics = pertaining to old age
USE = *

granular = grainy
USE = granular sugar

habitat = dwelling place
USE = destruction of wildlife habitat

hygienic = sanitary, clean
USE = It is not hygienic

illicit = Unlawful, illegal
USE = illicit liquor

illustrious = famous
USE = an illustrious political family

immaterial = irrelevant
USE = How you dress is immaterial for a written exam

immense = huge
USE = at immense cost

immerse = bathe, dip
USE = immerse something in water

impassioned = fiery, emotional
USE = to make an impassioned plea for something

imperative = vital, pressing
USE = it is imperative that I speak with him at once.

implant = instill
USE = He implanted some very strange attitudes in his children

imposing = intimidating, dignified
USE = an imposing figure

impressionable = susceptible, easily influenced
USE = at an impressionable age

impulse = sudden tendency
USE = a sudden impulse to shout

impulsive = to act suddenly
USE = Don't be so impulsive - think before you act.

inaugurate = to begin or start officially
USE = inaugurate a new shop

inconceivable = unthinkable
USE = It would be inconceivable for her to change her mind.

indulge = to give in to a craving or desire
USE = to indulge in a little nostalgia

inestimable = priceless
USE = The medical importance of this discovery is of inestimable value

infiltrate = to pass secretly into enemy territory
USE = A journalist managed to infiltrate the powerful drug cartel

infuriate = enrage, to anger
USE = His casual attitude infuriates me

integral = essential
USE = an integral part of

interrogate = to question formally
USE = Thousands of dissidents were interrogated

jaundiced = biased, embittered, affected by jaundice
USE = a very jaundiced view of life

keen = of sharp mind
USE = a keen interest

legible = readable
USE = his handwriting is barely legible

legislate = make laws
USE = *

legitimate = lawful
USE = The army must give power back to the legitimate government

lenient = forgiving, permissive
USE = They believe that judges are too lenient with terrorist suspects

linguistics = study of language
USE = *

logo = corporate symbol
USE = a corporate logo

malady = illness
USE = Apathy is one of the maladies of modern society

malice = spite, hatred
USE = There certainly wasn't any malice in her comments

marginal = insignificant
USE = a marginal improvement

martyr = sacrifice, symbol
USE = a religious martyr

matriculate = to enroll as a member of a college
USE = *

meager (BRITISH = meagre) = scanty
USE = a meager salary

melancholy = reflective, gloomy
USE = a melancholy piece of music

melodious = having a pleasing melody
USE = a melodious voice

monologue = dramatic speech performed by one actor
USE = *

negligible = insignificant
USE = negligible contribution

neutralize = offset, nullify, to balance
USE = to neutralize an acid

niche = nook, best position for something
USE = make a niche for himself

numismatics = coin collecting
USE = *

opine = think, to express an opinion
USE = Power grows from the barrel of a gun, opined Mao Tse-tung.

oracle = prophet
USE = Professor Jay is regarded as the oracle on eating disorders

oration = speech
USE = *

orator = speaker
USE = a skilled orator

orchestrate = organize
USE = a brilliantly orchestrated election campaign

ouster = ejection
USE = facing a possible ouster

pacify = appease, bring peace
USE = He pacified his crying child with a bottle

paradigm = a model
USE = to produce a change in the paradigm

paramount = chief, foremost, supreme
USE = of paramount importance

pathogenic = causing disease
USE = *

pauper = poor person
USE = *

pavilion = tent
USE = the West Pavilion of the General Hospital

pending = not decided
USE = The pending decision

perpetuity = eternity
USE = in perpetuity

phoenix = rebirth
USE = rose from the ashes like a phoenix

pilfer = steal
USE = He was caught pilfering from the shop

poach = steal game or fish
USE = to poach someone's ideas

porous = full of holes
USE = porous brick walls

posterior = rear, subsequent, bottom
USE = kindly move your posterior

predicament = difficult situation
USE = financial predicament

prescribe = urge, to recommend a treatment
USE = The drug is often prescribed for ulcers

prevalent = widespread
USE = These diseases are more prevalent among young children

procure = acquire
USE = He'd procured us seats in the front row

proficient = skillful, expert
USE = a proficient writer

progressive = advancing, liberal
USE = a progressive disease

proponent = supporter, advocate
USE = the leading proponents of

psychic = pertaining the psyche or mind
USE = psychic powers

quicken = revive, hasten
USE = to quicken the pace

radical = revolutionary, fundamental
USE = a radical thinker

rally = assemble
USE = an election rally

rapport = affinity, empathy, relationship of trust and respect
USE = to build rapport with someone

ration = allowance, portion
USE = no one was allowed more than their ration of food

rationale = justification
USE = the rationale behind some decision

rebuke = criticize
USE = He received a stern rebuke from the manager

receptive = open to other's ideas
USE = receptive to the idea

recount = to describe facts or events
USE = He recounted his adventures since he had left home

recruit = draftee
USE = to recruit volunteers

relent = soften, yield
USE = both sides refused to relent

remuneration = Compensation
USE = They demanded adequate remuneration for their work

renown = fame
USE = a woman of great renown

rent = tear, rupture
USE = There was a large rent in his parachute

repent = to regret a past action
USE = He repented of his sins

replicate = duplicate
USE = to replicate the original experiment

repress = suppress
USE = He repressed a sudden desire to cry

resolve = determination
USE = to strengthen your resolve for success

retain = keep
USE = She has lost her battle to retain control of the company

reticent = reserved
USE = the students were reticent about answering questions

retiring = modest, unassuming
USE = to be shy and retiring

revert = return
USE = the conversation reverted to money every five minutes

revoke = call back, cancel
USE = to revoke a decision

righteous = upright, moral
USE = a righteous and holy man

salutation = salute, greeting
USE = *

sanctuary = refuge
USE = a wildlife sanctuary

secluded = remote, isolated
USE = a secluded beach

sectarian = narrow-minded
USE = a sectarian murder

seismology = study of earthquakes
USE = *

sequel = continuation, epilogue
USE = the sequel of the movie Rocky is called Rocky II

sheepish = shy, timid
USE = a sheepish smile

skeptical (BRITISH = sceptical) = doubtful
USE = skeptical of his claims

sovereign = having supreme power
USE = a sovereign nation

spontaneous = impulsive
USE = spontaneous joy

stark = desolate, empty
USE = a stark room

stately = impressive, noble
USE = The procession moved through the village at a stately pace

stunted = arrested development
USE = stunted growth

subvert = undermine
USE = The rebel army was attempting to subvert the government

superfluous = overabundant
USE = superfluous comments

suspend = stop temporarily
USE = suspended for the day

syllabus = schedule
USE = Which books are on the syllabus this year

symposium = panel (discussion)
USE = a symposium on Indian cinema

synopsis = brief summary
USE = synopsis of her PhD thesis

tableau = scene, backdrop
USE = *

tactful = sensitive
USE = Mentioning his baldness wasn't very tactful

terminal = final, depot, station
USE = terminal cancer

thesaurus = book of synonyms
USE = a thesaurus in dictionary form

thesis = proposition, topic
USE = PhD thesis

tonal = pertaining to sound
USE = *

transitory = fleeting
USE = the transitory nature of life

unbridled = unrestrained
USE = unbridled enthusiasm

unfailing = steadfast, unfaltering
USE = her unfailing enthusiasm

unwarranted = unjustified
USE = unwarranted intrusions

utilitarian = pragmatic
USE = an ugly utilitarian building

voluble = talkative
USE = voluble praise

CD 11

ambulatory = able to walk, itinerant, related to walking around
USE = an ambulatory surgery

anachronistic = out of historical order, outdated
USE = He described the law as anachronistic

anthology = collection of literary works
USE = an anthology of modern quotations

antiquated = outdated, obsolete
USE = antiquated laws

antiquity = ancient times
USE = since antiquity

aquatic = pertaining to water
USE = aquatic plants

assonance = partial rhyme, resemblance in sound
USE = *

ballad = folk song, narrative poem
USE = *

belfry = bell tower
USE = *

belie = To misrepresent, expose as false
USE = Her calm face belied the terror she was feeling

bellow = shout, roar
USE = "Keep quiet!" the headmaster bellowed across the room

benchmark = standard of measure
USE = Her performance set a new benchmark

bequeath = to give or leave through will
USE = Her father bequeathed her the family fortune in his will

beseech = to beg, please, implore
USE = Stay a little longer, I beseech you!

bonanza = a stroke of luck, extremely large amount
USE = April was a bonanza month for car sales

boor = crude, vulgar person
USE = boorish

brigand = robber, bandit, outlaw
USE = *

bromide = cliché, a dull or commonplace person or idea
USE = *

cadence = rhythm, rhythmic flow of poetry, marching beat
USE = *

categorical = absolute, certain
USE = a categorical statement

cavalier = disdainful, nonchalant; carefree, happy
USE = that's a rather cavalier attitude.

cavort = to frolic, frisk
USE = They were spotted cavorting beside the swimming pool

cheeky = brass, forward, lacking prudence or discretion
USE = She's got such a cheeky grin

chortle = to chuckle, laugh, snort
USE = She chortled with glee at the news

concord = accord, agreement
USE = nations living in concord

confection = candy, something sweet to eat
USE = confectionery

connive = to conspire, scheme
USE = They connived to break the rules at every opportunity

cornucopia = cone-shaped horn filled with fruit, abundance
USE = cornucopia of every kind of food

corporeal = of the body, having to do with the body, tangible, material
USE = *

cosset = coddle, to pamper, treat with great care
USE = Children need to be cosseted

countervail = counterbalance, to exert force against
USE = countervailing duty on imports

covet = desire, to strongly desire something possessed by another
USE = the most coveted award

curt = abrupt, rude, blunt
USE = a curt reply

debunk = refute, expose, to discredit, disprove
USE = to debunk the myth

decathlon = athletic contest with ten events
USE = *

delectable = delicious, appetizing
USE = a delectable cake

demote = to reduce to a lower grade or rank
USE = The captain was demoted for failing to fulfill his duties

denude = strip bare, uncover, undress
USE = The countryside has been denuded by war

derisive = mocking, expressing ridicule or scorn
USE = derisive laughter

despot = tyrant, tyrannical ruler
USE = an evil despot

detractor = one who criticizes, one who takes something away
USE = His detractors claim that

disband = disperse, to break up
USE = She formed a political group which disbanded a year later

dispel = cause to banish, to drive out or scatter
USE = dispel doubts

dither = move without purpose
USE = Stop dithering and choose which one you want

doctrinaire = dogmatic, rigidly devoted to theories
USE = These principles are doctrinaire

dogged = persistent, stubborn
USE = ambition and dogged determination

doleful = sorrowful, sad
USE = a doleful expression

doting = attending, loving to excess
USE = photographs of the doting father with the baby on his knee

drivel = inane speech, stupid talk
USE = You're talking drivel as usual

dudgeon = resentment, indignant humor
USE = After waiting over an hour for them, he drove off in high dudgeon

dupe = fool, pawn, trick
USE = an innocent dupe

edict = order, law, command
USE = Most shops are ignoring the government's edict against Sunday trading

edifice = building
USE = The town hall is the only edifice surviving from the fifteenth century

efficacious = Effective, efficient
USE = efficacy

enchant = charm or attract
USE = an enchanting performance

encore = additional performance
USE = We were shouting for an encore

enmity = hostility, hatred
USE = She denied any personal enmity towards him

enshroud = cover
USE = Venus is enshrouded in thick clouds

entail = To involve; necessitate
USE = Such a large investment inevitably entails some risk

eon = indefinitely long period of time
USE = waiting eons for

ersatz = artificial
USE = ersatz chocolate made from carbo beans

estimable = meritorious, admirable
USE = He writes estimable poetry under a pseudonym

ethos = beliefs of a group
USE = national ethos

exalt = glorify, to elevate
USE = rose to the exalted position

expound = explain, to expand or increase
USE = He's always expounding on what's wrong with the world

farcical = absurd, ludicrous
USE = a farcical situation

feckless = incompetent, irresponsible, careless
USE = a feckless drunk

felicity = happiness
USE = the dubious felicity of marriage

fey = eccentric, whimsical, doomed
USE = dismiss as fey and frivolous

filibuster = long speech
USE = Conceivably, supporters of the law could filibuster to prevent it from being revised

forage = search for food
USE = The pigs foraged in the streets for food

forswear = deny
USE = to forswear alcohol

gnarled = deform
USE = a gnarled tree trunk

grievous = tragic, causing grief or sorrow
USE = Her death is a grievous loss to the nation

gyrate = to move in a circular motion
USE = A line of male dancers gyrated to the music while the audience screamed their appreciation

hardy = healthy
USE = A few hardy souls

harrowing = distressing
USE = a harrowing story

hegemony = authority, domination
USE = regional hegemony

heterodox = departing from established doctrines
USE = His opinions have always been distinctly heterodox

homonym = word identical in pronunciation but different in meaning
USE = 'No' and 'know' are homonyms

hymn = religious song
USE = a hymn book

hypothermia = low body temperature
USE = old people are dying needlessly of hypothermia

ilk = class, clan
USE = and others of their ilk

implicate = incriminate
USE = Have they any evidence to implicate him in the robbery

impound = seize and confine
USE = The police impounded cars

imprecation = curse, inculcate
USE = he walked along the street muttering imprecations

inculpate = accuse
USE = *

indelible = permanent
USE = indelible ink

indignant = resentment of injustice, angry
USE = He became very indignant when it was suggested he had made a mistake

infamy = shame
USE = the final infamy

ingress = entrance
USE = *

iniquity = sin, evil act
USE = the human injustice and iniquity

injunction = command, order
USE = The court issued an injunction to prevent the airline from increasing its prices

inquest = investigation
USE = An inquest is always held if murder is suspected

inquisitive = curious
USE = an inquisitive mind

interject = interrupt, insert
USE = That's ridiculous! Mary interjected

interpose = insert
USE = The teacher interposed herself between the two fighting boys

interregnum = interval between two successive reigns
USE = *

intersperse = to distribute among, mix with
USE = The documentary intersperses graphical animations with film clips of the actual event

inure = accustom, habituate, harden
USE = After spending some time on the island they became inured to the hardships

kudos = acclaim, fame, glory
USE = Being an actor has a certain amount of kudos attached to it

lament = mourn, grieve
USE = He lamented the decline in moral standards

laxity = carelessness
USE = any laxity will not be tolerated

leery = cautious, suspicious
USE = leery of authority figures

libertarian = one who believes in complete freedom
USE = Civil libertarians are worried about government censorship

lien = financial claim
USE = *

malinger = shirk, to evade responsibility by pretending to be ill
USE = is he really ill or just malingering

mar = damage, spoil
USE = Sadly, the text is marred by careless errors

megalith = ancient stone monument
USE = *

menagerie = zoo
USE = *

mendacity = untruth
USE = accused of mendacity

misconstrue = to misunderstand, fail to discover
USE = Their caution was misconstrued as cowardice

morsel = bite, piece, small bit of food
USE = a morsel of cheese

mutability = able to change
USE = *

mute = silent
USE = a mute child

nonchalant = casual, indifferent
USE = a nonchalant manner

nondescript = lacking distinctive features
USE = My office is in a nondescript building in the town

obliging = accommodating, considerate
USE = He found an obliging doctor

ontology = the study of the nature of existence
USE = *

overture = advance, proposal, musical introduction
USE = overtures of friendship.

overwrought = overworked, high-strung
USE = in an overwrought state

pare = peel, to trim
USE = Pare off any bits of the carrots that don't look very nice

parochial = provincial, a limited scope or outlook
USE = a parochial view

parole = conditional release of a prisoner
USE = released on parole

perplex = puzzle, bewilder
USE = The disease continues to perplex doctors

pestilence = disease
USE = vandalism is a pestilence which must be stamped out

picayune = trifling, petty
USE = The misery suffered in this war makes your own problems seem pretty picayune

piety = devoutness
USE = *

plaintive = expressing sorrow
USE = the plaintive sound of the bagpipes

plaudit = acclaim
USE = She's received plaudits for her work with homeless people

pliant = supple, flexible
USE = toys are made of pliant rubber

plucky = courageous
USE = It was plucky of you to chase after the burglar

plummet = fall
USE = House prices have plummeted in recent months

pontificate = to speak at length
USE = to pontificate about

posit = to put in position
USE = If we posit that wage rises cause inflation, it follows that we should try to minimize them

precis = summary
USE = a précis of the report

predestine = to decide in advance
USE = *

predicate = to found or base on
USE = subject and predicate

prepossessing = appealing, charming, attractive
USE = a very prepossessing sort of person

pretentious = affected, inflated, showy
USE = a pretentious art critic

prologue = introduction
USE = A series of internal struggles was the prologue to full-scale civil war

protagonist = main character in a story
USE = *

providential = fortunate, lucky
USE = a providential opportunity

provocation = incitement to act or respond
USE = He'd fly into a rage at the slightest provocation

prowess = strength, expertise, bravery, skill
USE = sporting prowess

pugilism = boxing
USE = *

pulverize = crush, destroy
USE = pulverized coal

puritanical = adhering to a rigid moral code
USE = He rebelled against his puritanical upbringing

quiver = tremble, vibrate
USE = Her bottom lip quivered and tears started in his eyes

quotidian = occurring daily
USE = TV has become part of our quotidian existence

rash = hasty, brash, careless
USE = a rash decision

ratify = approve, confirm
USE = ratified the UN convention

reclusive = solitary
USE = a reclusive genius, he did not give interviews

rejoinder = answer, retort, response
USE = a witty rejoinder to the question

remit = forgive, send payment
USE = He remitted half his salary to his parents

renascent = reborn
USE = *

repose = relaxation
USE = She reposed on the sofa.

reprise = repetition
USE = *

repulse = repel
USE = The enemy attack was quickly repulsed.

resolute = determined
USE = Their resolute opposition

respire = breathe
USE = *

rhapsody = emotional literary or musical work
USE = *

riposte = a retort
USE = a witty riposte

rue = regret
USE = *

salacious = licentious
USE = a salacious film

savory (BRITISH = savoury) = agreeable in taste or smell
USE = savory pancakes

scabrous = difficult
USE = The book includes some memorably seedy characters and scabrous descriptions

secede = withdraw
USE = to secede from a country.

seminal = fundamental
USE = a seminal article

senescent = aging, growing old
USE = *

sentient = conscious
USE = a sentient person

shard = piece of broken glass or pottery
USE = Shards of glass

shirk = to avoid a task due to laziness or fear
USE = to shirk one's responsibilities

sidle = move sideways
USE = She sidled past him, pretending that she had not seen him

singe = to burn slightly
USE = start to singe

smelt = refine metal
USE = smelter

snippet = morsel, tiny part
USE = I heard an interesting snippet

soluble = dissolvable
USE = soluble aspirin

sophistry = specious reasoning, clever use of false reasoning that seems to be true
USE = *

stifle = suppress
USE = such laws stifle creativity

stratify = form into layers
USE = the names were stratified by age and gender

striated = to stripe
USE = the crayon walls were striated with color

stupefy = deaden, dumfound
USE = *

stylize (BRITISH = stylise) = formalize
USE = *

subterranean = underground, hidden
USE = a subterranean river

sullen = sulky, sour
USE = sullen resentment

supererogatory = wanton, superfluous
USE = *

supervise = oversee the work of others
USE = The children play while two teachers supervise

taint = pollute
USE = His reputation was permanently tainted

tandem = two or more things together
USE = in tandem

tang = strong taste
USE = the tang of the sea air

tangential = peripheral
USE = *

tangible = touchable
USE = tangible benefits

tempestuous = agitated, stormy
USE = a tempestuous marriage

tenable = defensible, valid
USE = His theory is no longer tenable

testament = covenant, will
USE = the old testament

tidings = news, information
USE = tidings of great joy

torsion = twisting
USE = *

trounce = thrash, defeat
USE = She trounced her rivals in the election

troupe = group of actors
USE = a dance troupe

tyrannical = dictatorial
USE = a tyrannical leader

unavailing = useless, futile
USE = the efforts have so far proved unavailing

unfrock = discharge
USE = *

unstinting = generous
USE = unstinting support

valiant = brave
USE = a valiant effort

vanquish = conquer
USE = The vanquished army surrendered their weapons

veracity = Truthfulness
USE = the veracity of her alibi was in question because

vestige = trace
USE = These old buildings are the last vestiges of a colonial past

veto = reject
USE = US, Russia and others could veto the proposal in the UN

viaduct = waterway
USE = a railway viaduct

vigilant = on guard
USE = to be extra vigilant

vindictive = Revengeful
USE = a vindictive former prisoner

vivid = lifelike, clear
USE = a vivid imagination

woe = deep suffering or grief
USE = her face was lined and full of woe

writ = written document
USE = writ petition

CD 12

analgesia = pain reducer
USE = analgesic

antagonist = an opponent, rival, adversary
USE = the antagonist was finally defeated

applause = acclaim, cheering, clapping, praise
USE = a round of applause

apprehension = fear, anxiety
USE = it's normal to feel a little apprehension before an exam

appropriate = to take or steal something
USE = appropriate someone's wealth

aspire = hope to achieve something
USE = aspire to be a cricketer

atrocious = extremely bad, wicked, monstrous
USE = atrocious weather or atrocious behavior

attainment = achievement
USE = *

audacious = Fearless, bold, daring
USE = an audacious claim

audible = Loud enough to be heard
USE = audible music

auditory = related to hearing
USE = the auditory areas of the brain

avenge = to take revenge or retaliate
USE = He swore he would avenge his brother's death.

ban = prohibition
USE = a ban on alcohol in Gujarat

beneficial = helpful, advantageous
USE = physical exercise is beneficial for your health

bereaved = suffering death of a loved one
USE = bereaved parents

bias = partiality, prejudice, slant
USE = biased opinion

bibliophile = One who loves books
USE = *

blaspheme = curse, profane, irreverent
USE = *

botanical = Connected with the study or cultivation of plants
USE = botanical garden

botany = The science of plants
USE = *

bouquet = a bunch of flowers
USE = gift a bouquet on birthday

cartography = the science or art of making maps
USE = *

celebrity = fame, widespread acclaim
USE = a film celebrity

certitude = assurance, confidence of certainty
USE = *

chaos = utter disorder and confusion
USE = The country's at war and everything is in chaos

chromatic = relating to color
USE = photo-chromatic sunglasses

circumference = The boundary-line of a circle
USE = the circumference of a circle

civil = courteous and polite
USE = He and his ex-wife can't even have a civil conversation

coerce = to force
USE = Employees said they were coerced into signing the agreement

cognition = understanding, perception
USE = it is important to learn about human memory and cognition

coherent = understandable, clear, logical, lucid
USE = coherent argument

concern = a matter of importance
USE = *

concerto = A musical composition for orchestra
USE = a piano concerto by Mozart

congress = formal meeting or assembly
USE = *

corrode = To ruin or destroy
USE = Steel tends to corrode faster in a salty atmosphere

cosmetic = related to the art of beautifying
USE = cosmetic surgery

credible = Believable, plausible
USE = credible evidence

defendant = person required to answer a legal suit
USE = *

deficient = Not having adequate supply, defective
USE = A diet deficient in vitamin D

deflation = decrease, depreciation
USE = *

deform = To disfigure, distort
USE = Age deforms the spine.

delineation = the act of representing pictorially, depiction
USE = *

delta = an alluvial deposit at the mouth of a stream
USE = the delta of the Nile

demotion = lowering in rank or grade
USE = demotion vs. promotion

denunciation = public condemnation
USE = *

dialect = regional style of speaking
USE = a regional dialect

differentiate = to distinguish between two items
USE = We do not differentiate between our workers on the basis of

diplomacy = Tact or skill in social matters, discretion
USE = It took all her tact and diplomacy to persuade him not to resign

disclose = reveal, to confess, divulge
USE = The police have disclosed that two officers are under internal investigation

discredit = to dishonor or disgrace
USE = discredited theories

disregard = pay no attention to
USE = complete disregard for

divert = to turn from one course to another
USE = to divert attention

dowry = property which a wife brings in marriage
USE = dowry deaths have not fully stopped yet

duration = The period of time
USE = of two years' duration

ecstatic = joyful
USE = an ecstatic crowd

effervescent = Giving off bubbles of gas
USE = effervescent vitamin C tablets

embezzle = to steal money in violation of a trust
USE = She embezzled thousands of dollars from the charity

endurance = ability to withstand hardships
USE = a test of human endurance

evict = to put out or force out
USE = Tenants who fall behind in their rent risk being evicted

exhilarate = To fill with high or cheerful spirits
USE = riding motorcycle is an exhilarating experience

explode = to disprove, blow up
USE = A bomb exploded

fabricated = constructed, invented
USE = a fabricated story

feud = a war between two people or groups
USE = a family feud

flag = to loose energy and strength
USE = The conversation was flagging

flounder = to falter, waver
USE = Although his business was a success, his marriage was floundering

forethought = Premeditation
USE = I had the forethought to make a copy of the letter

frivolous = Trivial
USE = I feel like doing something completely frivolous today

gestation = Pregnancy
USE = The period of gestation

gradation = A step, degree, rank
USE = the gradations of a ruler

hectic = hasty, hurried
USE = a hectic schedule

hemorrhage (BRITISH = haemorrhage) = heavy bleeding
USE = a brain hemorrhage

holistic = as a whole
USE = a holistic approach to disease

hypochondria = morbid anxiety about health, imaginary illness
USE = I thought the doctor was going to accuse me of hypochondria

hypocrite = One who makes false professions of his views
USE = He's a hypocrite

hypothesis = assumption subject to proof
USE = Several hypotheses for global warming have been suggested

impoverish = To make indigent or poor
USE = Excessive farming had impoverished the soil

indefensible = Untenable, unforgivable
USE = The war is morally indefensible

induct = To bring in
USE = was inducted into the party

industry = business or trade, energy
USE = *

inebriated = drunk, intoxicated
USE = inebriated state

inglorious = Shameful
USE = a long, inglorious record

ingrained = deeply established, firmly rooted
USE = The belief that you should own your own house is deeply ingrained in our society

inhabit = to occupy, to dwell in
USE = These remote islands are inhabited only by birds and small animals

inject = To introduce, as a fluid, by injection
USE = to inject himself with insulin every day

innumerable = Countless
USE = innumerable problems

insubstantial = lacking substance, insignificant
USE = insubstantial evidence

insufficiency = lacking in something
USE = *

intersect = To cut through so as to divide
USE = The roads intersect near the bridge

intrusion = entering without invitation; encroachment
USE = excessive government intrusion

invariable = Unchangeable
USE = The menu is invariable but the food is always good

juvenile = young, childish acting
USE = juvenile crime

kernel = A grain or seed, essential part
USE = a kernel of truth

larynx = organ containing vocal cords
USE = *

lethargy = indifferent, inactivity
USE = *

literal = word for word
USE = The literal meaning

locomotion = moving from one place to another
USE = *

luxuriance = elegance, lavishness
USE = *

malevolent = causing evil or harm to others
USE = I could feel his malevolent gaze

mannered = affected, artificial
USE = the actor was criticized for being very mannered

materialism = preoccupation with physical comforts
USE = we are becoming a self-centered society, preoccupied with materialism

medieval = relating to the middle ages
USE = a medieval building

metronome = time keeping device used in music
USE = *

monochromatic = having only one color
USE = *

monogamy = marriage to one person at a time
USE = *

monolith = large block of stone
USE = *

naïve = simple, ingenuous
USE = It was a little naive of you

narrative = account, story
USE = It's a moving narrative of wartime adventure

negligent = careless, inattentive
USE = the teacher had been negligent in allowing the children to swim in dangerous water

noble = illustrious, imperial, legendary
USE = a noble gesture

offshoot = branch
USE = an offshoot of

paradoxical = self-contradictory but true
USE = this statement appears paradoxical

paternity = Fatherhood
USE = paternity leave

peer = a person of the same rank or group
USE = peer pressure

penultimate = next to last
USE = It's the penultimate episode of the series tonight

pervasive = Thoroughly penetrating or permeating
USE = a pervasive smell of diesel

pervert = to cause to change in immoral way, to misuse
USE = Her ideas have been shamelessly perverted to serve the president's propaganda campaign

philanthropy = generosity to worthy causes
USE = *

phonic = related to the nature of sound
USE = *

pneumatic = related to of air or gas
USE = pneumatic brakes

polarized (BRITISH = polarize) = split into opposite extremes or camps
USE = The debate is becoming polarized

pompous = self-important
USE = He can sometimes sound a bit pompous when he talks about acting

pore = to study closely or meditatively
USE = She spends her evenings poring over textbooks

precision = state of being precise, exactness
USE = Great precision is required to align the mirrors accurately

preface = introduction to a book
USE = *

procrastination = Delay
USE = *

protrusion = The act of protruding
USE = It has a series of protrusions along its back

qualify = to provide with needed skills
USE = B.Ed. qualifies you to teach in any secondary school.

rapt = deeply absorbed
USE = The children watched with rapt attention

redundancy = Excess
USE = *

reflection = image, thought
USE = reflection in a pool of water

reform = Change for the better
USE = who will reform India's obsolete laws

regress = return to a former place or condition
USE = regressed to the mental age of a five-year-old

repeal = no further effect
USE = repeal a law

repel = repulse, disgust, offend
USE = She was repelled by his ugliness

resonate = to echo
USE = His voice resonated in the empty building

retract = To recall or take back
USE = retract an invitation

sap = diminish, undermine
USE = Constant criticism saps you of your confidence

scale = climb up, ascend
USE = The prisoner scaled the high prison wall and ran off

scarcity = not enough, insufficient
USE = the scarcity of skilled workers

scenario = plot outline, screenplay
USE = There are several possible scenarios

slight = Of a small importance
USE = a slight improvement

submissive = yielding, timid
USE = a quiet submissive wife

subtle = Discriminating
USE = a subtle shade of pink

superabundance = An excessive amount
USE = *

supposition = assumption
USE = based on pure supposition

testimonial = A formal token of regard, often presented in public
USE = I have thousands of testimonials from my students about how they benefited greatly

theology = study of God and religion
USE = *

theoretical = abstract
USE = theoretical physics

tolerance = capacity to respect different values
USE = religious tolerance

tranquil = Calm
USE = a tranquil rural setting

transcendent = Surpassing
USE = transcendent power

transcript = A copy made directly from an original
USE = Mysteriously, the transcript of what was said at the trial went missing

transgress = To break a law
USE = anyone who transgresses will be severely punished

unruffled = calm, not anxious
USE = For a man in imminent danger of losing his job, he appeared quite unruffled

uproarious = Noisy
USE = an uproarious debate

variable = changeable
USE = variable interest rate

withdrawn = introverted, remote, timid
USE = she became quiet and withdrawn and rarely went out

toxin = poison
USE = toxins cause diseases

trammel = An impediment
USE = *

transfiguration = a change, an exalting change
USE = *

transformation = a change in form or appearance
USE = I'd never seen him in smart evening clothes before - it was quite a transformation

translation = a change from one state to another
USE = A literal translation

trifling = of slight worth, trivial
USE = a trifling sum of money

trying = difficult to deal with
USE = I've had a very trying day at work

unadulterated = absolutely pure
USE = *hint

unappealing = unattractive
USE = *

unbending = inflexible, unyielding
USE = a stern and unbending politician

undaunted = resolute even in adversity
USE = The team remains undaunted, despite three defeats in a row

undocumented = not certified
USE = *

undulating = moving in waves
USE = undulating roads

unfettered = liberated, free from chains
USE = In writing poetry, one is unfettered by the normal rules of sentence structure

ungracious = rude, disagreeable
USE = *

unheralded = unannounced, unexpected
USE = *

unidimensional = having one size or dimension
USE = *

uniform = consistent and unchanging
USE = the walls and furniture are a uniform gray

uninitiated = not familiar with an area of study
USE = *

unpolished = lacking sophistication
USE = *

unscrupulous = dishonest
USE = an unscrupulous financial adviser

unsoiled = clean, pure
USE = *

unsolicited = not requested
USE = unsolicited advice

unswayable = unable to change
USE = *

untrammeled (BRITISH = untrammelled) = unhampered
USE = Self-governing schools are untrammeled by education authority rules

unyielding = firm, resolute
USE = unyielding in its demands

upsurge = an increase, rise
USE = An upsurge in violence

valorous = Courageous, brave
USE = *

vehemently = strongly, urgently
USE = vehemently denied

veneration = adoration, honor
USE = Gandhi became an object of widespread veneration

verdure = fresh, rich vegetation
USE = *

verified = proven true
USE = Under interrogation, she verified that the tapes were authentic

vermin = A noxious animal
USE = He thought all terrorists were vermin

verve = enthusiasm, liveliness
USE = She delivered her speech with tremendous wit and verve

vim = energy, enthusiasm
USE = At 87, she is still full of vim and vigor

vindication = clearance from blame or suspicion
USE = the victory is being seen as a vindication of their tactics

virginal = pure, chaste
USE = virginal innocence

virtue = conforming to what is right
USE = Patience is a virtue

vituperate = to abuse verbally
USE = *

void = not legally enforceable, empty
USE = The election was declared null and void

volley = flight of missiles
USE = a fresh volley of machine-gun fire

vortex = swirling, resembling a whirlpool
USE = I was sucked into a vortex of despair

vulgar = obscene
USE = a vulgar patterned shirt

waspish = rude, behaving badly
USE = a waspish tongue

waver = to show indecision
USE = my concentration began to waver as lunch approached

wayward = erratic, reckless
USE = *

weighty = important, momentous
USE = weighty matters

whimsy = playful or fanciful idea
USE = *

zoologist = scientist who studies animals
USE = *

CD 13

alienated = distanced, estranged
USE = All these changes to the newspaper have alienated its traditional readers

aligned = committed to one side or party
USE = non-aligned movement

allocation = allowance, portion, share
USE = the allocation of resources

animation = enthusiasm, excitement
USE = She spoke with great animation about her latest discoveries

antecedent = coming before in place or time
USE = find out about their antecedents

antedate = dated prior to the actual occurrence
USE = antedated document

antepenultimate = third from last
USE = *

anterior = before, prior, preceding
USE = anterior and posterior

apace = done quickly
USE = The project is coming on apace

aphelion = a point in planet's orbits that is farthest from Sun
USE = *

apostrophe = speech to the reader; the superscript sign
USE = *

arbitrator = mediator, negotiator
USE = *

arboreal = related to trees
USE = arboreal animals

arboretum = A botanical garden of trees or shrubs
USE = *

asocial = unable or unwilling to interact socially
USE = *

assignation = appointment for lover's meeting
USE = *

assimilation = act of blending in, becoming similar
USE = the assimilation of people of Indian origin in the US is a slow process

base = being of low value or position
USE = I accused him of having base motives

bay = to bark especially deep prolonged way
USE = the Bay of Bengal

becalm = To make calm, quiet, still
USE = *hint

becloud = to confuse, darken with clouds
USE = *hint

bemuse = to confuse, stupefy
USE = He seemed bemused by all the attention

beneficent = Characterized by charity and kindness
USE = a beneficent aunt

besmear = To smear
USE = *

betoken = to indicate, signify, give evidence of
USE = *

billet = board or lodging for troops
USE = Our billets were about a mile out of town

bisect = to cut into two parts
USE = The new road will bisect the town

bluster = to boast or make threats loudly
USE = You had no right to do it, no right at all, he blustered.

bonhomie = good natured, geniality
USE = *

bursar = treasurer
USE = *

bustle = To hurry, commotion, energetic activity
USE = There were lots of shoppers bustling about

butt = person or a thing that is object of ridicule
USE = being the butt of their jokes

byway = back road
USE = *

canonize = to declare a person a saint; raise to highest honors
USE = *

carom = to strike and rebound
USE = we play carom

cast = copy or replica
USE = *

caulk = to make watertight
USE = *

causality = cause-and-effect relationship
USE = cause

charm = compelling attractiveness
USE = a woman of great charm

choice = specially selected, preferred
USE = our pizza uses only choice ingredients

chronicler = one who keeps records of historical events
USE = *

circumnavigate = To sail completely around
USE = They circumnavigated the world

cistern = tank for rainwater
USE = we just installed a cistern in the toilet

civility = courtesy, politeness
USE = After a few civilities, they got down to business

clement = mild
USE = It's very clement for the time of year

cloying = indulging in excess
USE = the cloying sentimentality of the film

collected = acting calm and composed
USE = she remained calm and collected

comeliness = physical grace and beauty
USE = *hint

commonplace = ordinary, found every day
USE = Home computers are increasingly commonplace

communicable = transmittable
USE = communicable disease

compendious = summarizing completely and briefly
USE = *

compunctious = feeling guilty or having misgivings
USE = *

conceptualize (BRITISH = conceptualise) = to envision, imagine
USE = can you conceptualize a new solution

conglomerate = collected group of varied things
USE = an industrial conglomerate

congruity = correspondence, harmony, agreement
USE = *

conjoin = to join together
USE = conjoined twins

considerable = significant, worth considering
USE = The fire caused considerable damage

consistent = containing no contradictions, being harmonious
USE = a consistent improvement

constant = completely uniform and unchanging
USE = a fairly constant speed

constrict = restricted, to inhibit
USE = The blood vessels constricted.

contradict = to deny or oppose
USE = He kept contradicting himself

convalescence = gradual recovery after an illness
USE = *

corpulence = obesity, fatness, bulkiness
USE = *

cosmography = The science of the universe
USE = *

coven = group of witches
USE = *

cutlery = cutting instruments, tableware
USE = crockery and cutlery

cygnet = A young swan
USE = *

cynic = person who distrusts the motives of others
USE = I'm too much of a cynic to believe that he'll keep his promise

decamp = To leave suddenly or unexpectedly
USE = He decamped from the hotel with someone else's luggage

defamatory = slanderous, injurious to the reputation
USE = the remarks were highly defamatory

defect = an imperfection or shortcoming
USE = birth defects

deferential = respectful and polite in a submissive way
USE = deferential to anyone in authority

demarcation = a boundary or distinction
USE = the line of demarcation

demystify = to remove mystery from, clarify
USE = demystify the workings of

derive = To deduce, as from a premise
USE = She derives great pleasure from playing the violin

derogate = to belittle, disparage
USE = *hint

detestation = extreme hatred
USE = *

deviation = departure, exception
USE = Any deviation from the party's faith is seen as betrayal

differ = disagree
USE = I beg to differ

diffract = to cause light to separate into parts
USE = *

diffuse = widely spread out
USE = Television is a powerful means of diffusing knowledge

diluvia = relating to a flood
USE = *

diminutive = small
USE = a diminutive figure

disaffected = discontented and disloyal
USE = steps to attract disaffected voters

disbar = to expel from legal profession
USE = *hint

discern = to perceive something obscure
USE = I could just discern a figure in the darkness

discompose = to disturb the composure or serenity
USE = *

disconcerting = bewildering, perplexing, slightly disturbing
USE = There was a disconcerting silence

discredited = disbelieved, discounted, disgraced, dishonored
USE = discredited theories

discretionary = subject to one's own judgment
USE = Judges have great discretionary powers

disdainful = contemptuous, scornful
USE = a disdainful expression

disengaged = disconnected, disassociated
USE = to disengage your emotions from

disgorge = vomit, throw up, discharge violently
USE = The pipe was found to be disgorging dangerous chemicals into the sea

disheveled (BRITISH = dishevelled) = ruffled, untidy, unkempt
USE = disheveled appearance

disinclined = averse, unwilling, lacking desire
USE = I feel disinclined to offer him a job

disinterest = lack of interest or a disadvantage
USE = a disinterested person can act as a mediator

dispense = to distribute, administer
USE = a vending machine on the platform dispenses snacks

dispense with = to suspend the operation of, do without
USE = They've had to dispense with a lot of luxuries since her husband lost his job

disquieted = feeling anxiety, being disturbed, lacking peace
USE = The leader's decline in popularity is causing disquiet among supporters

dissension = difference of opinion
USE = signs of dissension within the party

dissociate = to separate, remove from an association
USE = I can't dissociate the man from his political opinions

dissonant = Harsh and unpleasant sounding
USE = *

diurnal = Daily
USE = diurnal vs. nocturnal

dolor (BRITISH = dolour) = Lamentation, sadness
USE = *

dotard = senile old person
USE = *

draft = to plan, to recruit, conscript
USE = a rough draft

draw = to attract, to pull toward
USE = to draw attention

dumb = unable to speak
USE = She was struck dumb by what she had seen

durability = strength, sturdiness
USE = the durability of the materials used

eddy = swirling current of water, air etc,
USE = The water eddied around in a whirlpool

elegy = A lyric poem lamenting the dead
USE = *

elevated = high in status, exalted
USE = a more elevated position

emotive = appealing to or expressing emotion
USE = a highly emotive issue

encipher = to translate a message into code
USE = *

endogamous = marrying within a specific group due to law or custom
USE = *

entomologist = scientist who studies insects
USE = *

epigraph = quotation at the beginning of a literary work
USE = *

epochal = very significant or influential, defining an epoch or time period
USE = an epochal speech by the President

esurient = hungry, greedy
USE = *

euphony = Agreeableness of sound
USE = *

eurhythmics = art of harmonious bodily movement
USE = *

evident = clear, able to be understood
USE = self-evident

exigent = Urgent
USE = an exigent problem

expire = to come to an end, die, breathe out
USE = our license expires next month

explicable = capable of being explained
USE = what he said was quite explicable

exponent = one who champions or advocates
USE = an exponent of free trade

extinction = end of a living thing or species
USE = The extinction of the dinosaurs

famine = extreme scarcity of food
USE = a widespread famine

fault = break in a rock formation, mistake
USE = It's not my fault she didn't come

fawn = to flatter excessively, seek the favor of
USE = *

faze = to bother, upset, or disconcert
USE = No one is fazed by the sight of guns here any more

federation = union of state or organization
USE = The United States is a federation of 50 individual states

feisty = excitable, easily drawn into quarrels
USE = a feisty lady

fictive = fictional, imaginary
USE = *hint

fiendish = excessively bad or cruel
USE = a fiendish attack

fission = break
USE = nuclear fission

fixity = being fixed or stable
USE = *

flammable = combustible, being easily burned
USE = petrol is highly flammable

flurried = to become agitated and confused
USE = *

fodder = coarse food for the cattle, horses etc
USE = *hint

foliate = to grow, sprout leaves
USE = *

ford = place where a river can be crossed on foot
USE = *

foreboding = sense of evil to come
USE = He had a strange foreboding something would go wrong

forefend = to prevent
USE = *

forensic = study of argumentation and debate
USE = forensic evidence

forestall = to prevent, delay, anticipate
USE = The government forestalled criticism

forlorn = neglected, forsaken
USE = She looked a forlorn figure standing at the bus stop

formulate = to conceive, devise
USE = to formulate legislation

fortnight = two weeks
USE = a fortnight ago

foundation = groundwork, support, institution
USE = the foundation of a new state

fragmentation = division
USE = fragmentation of the group

frank = honest and straightforward
USE = a full and frank discussion

fratricide = murder of a brother
USE = *

fraud = deception, hoax
USE = fraud charges

gallant = a very fashionable young man
USE = a gallant effort

game = courageous
USE = It was a difficult challenge, but he was game

gaucherie = a tactless or awkward act
USE = *

gavel = mallet or hammer used for commanding attention
USE = *

girth = circumferential measure of thickness
USE = The tree was 2 meters in girth

global = involving the entire world, relating to a whole
USE = a global catastrophe

gluttony = eating and drinking to excess
USE = They treat Christmas as just another excuse for gluttony

Gnostic = having to do with knowledge
USE = *

grandiloquence = pompous talk, fancy but meaningless language
USE = *

grasp = to perceive and understand, to hold securely
USE = to grasp the main points

grimy = dirty, filthy
USE = The child's face was grimy

gross = total before deductions
USE = gross profit

grubby = dirty, sloppy
USE = a grubby T-shirt

hail = a greeting
USE = *

hamlet = small village
USE = *

harmony = accord, agreement
USE = religious harmony, racial harmony

hasten = to speed up
USE = poor medical treatment hastened her death

headlong = hasty, rash
USE = The car skidded and plunged headlong over the cliff

headstrong = insisting on one's own way
USE = She was a headstrong child, always getting into trouble

heathen = hurried, confused
USE = *

hector = a bully
USE = *

heighten = to raise
USE = heightened the tension

hemicycle = semicircular form or structure
USE = *

heretical = opposed to an established religious orthodoxy
USE = Her belief that a split would be good for the party was regarded as heretical

hidebound = excessively rigid, dry and stiff
USE = *hint

hinder = To obstruct
USE = hindered firefighters in their efforts

hindsight = perception of events after they happen
USE = In hindsight, it would have been better to wait

hinterland = wilderness
USE = *

honor (BRITISH = honour) = to praise, glorify, pay tribute to
USE = guest of honor

husband = to farm, manage carefully
USE = animal husbandry

hutch = pen, or wood or wire box for animals
USE = a rabbit hutch

hydrate = to add water to
USE = *hint

hyperventilate = to breathe abnormally fast
USE = *

idealism = pursuit of noble goals
USE = youthful idealism

ignoramus = an ignorant person
USE = I'm a complete ignoramus where computers are concerned.

immunological = related to immune system
USE = an immunological disease

impose = to inflict, force upon
USE = imposed a ban on alcohol

impudent = arrogant and rude
USE = an impudent remark

incarceration = imprisonment
USE = *

inclination = tendency towards
USE = My own inclination would be to look for another job

inextricable = incapable of being disentangled
USE = for many, legend and truth are often inextricable

infatuated = inspired with foolish passion
USE = he was infatuated with his boss

infuriating = provoking anger or outrage
USE = such attitude infuriates me

innateness = state of being natural
USE = *

inoffensive = harmless, innocent
USE = an inoffensive article

inoperable = not operable, incurable by surgery
USE = *hint

insentient = unfeeling, unconscious
USE = *hint

insoluble = not able to be solved or explained
USE = an insoluble problem

intemperate = not moderate
USE = an intemperate outburst

interlocutor = someone taking part in a dialogue
USE = to act as interpreter and interlocutor

intimation = clue, suggestion
USE = the first intimation

intramural = Situated within the walls of a city
USE = an intramural basketball competition

intrigued = interested, internal
USE = intrigued by the question of

intuitive = instinctive, untaught
USE = an intuitive approach

investiture = ceremony conferring authority
USE = *

inviolable = safe from violation or assault
USE = Everyone has an inviolable right to protection by a fair legal system

irresolvable = unable to be resolved, not analyzable
USE = *hint

jangling = clashing, harshly unpleasant
USE = the jangling of bells

jibe = to make taunting remarks
USE = She jibed constantly at the way he ran his business

jubilee = special anniversary
USE = silver jubilee

juxtaposition = placing close together
USE = the juxtaposition of two very different cultures

CD 14

keynote = main idea of a speech, program
USE = a keynote address

laceration = cut or wound
USE = signs of laceration and bruising

lambaste = disapprove angrily
USE = His first novel was well and truly lambasted by the critics

languid = Relaxed, slow, indifferent
USE = a languid manner

lap = to drink using the tongue, to wash against
USE = The waves gently lapped the shore

larder = pantry, place where food is kept
USE = a well-stocked larder

levitate = to rise in the air or cause to rise
USE = *

liberal = tolerant, broad-minded
USE = a liberal society

liberation = freedom, emancipation
USE = the liberation of India from the British rule

license = freedom to act
USE = driver's license

liniment = medicinal liquid used externally to ease pain
USE = *

literate = able to read and write
USE = computer literate

lodged = fixed in one position
USE = A fish bone had lodged in her throat

low = to make a sound like a cow, moo
USE = *hint

lumber = move heavily or clumsily
USE = a herd of elephants lumbering across the plain

luminary = bright object
USE = Luminaries of stage and screen

lurk = to lie in wait, to be concealed
USE = Someone was lurking in the shadows

lyrical = suitable for poetry and song, expressing feeling
USE = lyrical descriptions

macrobiotics = art of prolonging life by special diet of organic, nonmeat substances
USE = *

macrocosm = The whole of any system
USE = *

mainstay = chief support
USE = Cattle farming is the mainstay of the country's economy

malfunction = breakdown, failure
USE = the pilot had reported a malfunction of the aircraft's navigation system.

malnutrition = undernourishment
USE = suffering from severe malnutrition

manual = hand-operated, physical
USE = the manual sorting of letters

manumission = release from slavery
USE = *

masquerade = disguise, action that conceals the truth
USE = the masquerade of being happily married

matrilineal = tracing ancestry through mother's line rather than father's
USE = *

meaningful = significant
USE = I am looking for meaningful work

meddler = person interfering in others' affairs
USE = *

melody = pleasing musical sounds, tune
USE = His songs are always strong on melody

meridian = circle passing through the two poles of the earth
USE = The prime meridian of longitude is in Greenwich

meritorious = deserving reward of praise
USE = an award for meritorious service

microbe = micro organism
USE = *

minimal = smallest in amount, least possible
USE = the accident caused minimal damage

misapprehend = To misunderstand
USE = *

miserliness = extreme stinginess
USE = *

mobility = ease of movement
USE = total loss of mobility

mock = to deride, ridicule
USE = She made fun of him by mocking his limp

moderate = reasonable, not extreme
USE = a moderate in the party

mollusk (BRITISH = mollusc) = sea animal with a soft body
USE = Oysters are mollusks, as are snails

montage = composite picture
USE = a montage of images

mordacious = Biting or giving to biting
USE = *

mottle = to mark with spots
USE = *

multifaceted = having many parts, many-sided
USE = a multi-faceted business

munitions = ammunition
USE = a munitions factory

neonate = newborn child
USE = *

neutrality = disinterest, impartiality
USE = political neutrality

niggling = trifle, petty worry
USE = a niggling doubt

notoriety = unfavorable fame
USE = He gained notoriety for murdering eleven women

novitiate = period of being a beginner or novice
USE = *

nutritive = relating to nutrition or health
USE = Chemical sweeteners have no nutritional value

oblivious = unaware, inattentive
USE = she was totally oblivious of her surroundings

obscurity = place of thing that's hard to perceive
USE = he came back from obscurity and became famous again

obsessive = preoccupying, all-consuming
USE = obsessive behavior

ostracism = exclusion, temporary banishment
USE = social ostracism and discrimination

overabundance = excess, surfeit
USE = *

overstate = to embellish, exaggerate
USE = The impact of the new legislation has been greatly overstated

pacific = calm, peaceful
USE = *hint

paleontology (BRITISH = palaeontology) = science of ancient life and fossil organisms
USE = *

palisade = fence made up of stakes
USE = *

palpitation = trembling, shaking, irregular beating
USE = increased palpitation

parch = to dry or shrivel
USE = parched land

parsimony = stinginess
USE = *

peerless = Of unequaled excellence or worth
USE = peerless beauty

pen = penitentiary
USE = *

perambulate = To walk about
USE = *

percipient = One who or that which perceives
USE = *hint

peregrinate = to wander from place to place
USE = *

perihelion = point in orbit nearest to the sun
USE = *

periphrastic = containing too many words
USE = *

perjure = to tell a lie under oath
USE = The judge warned the witness not to perjure herself

personification = act of attributing human qualities to objects
USE = personification of evil

perspicacious = shrewd, astute, keen-witted
USE = His perspicacious grandfather had bought the land as an investment,

pettish = fretful
USE = *

petulance = impatient capricious, rudeness
USE = *

phalanx = massed group of soldiers, people, or things
USE = Bodyguards formed a solid phalanx around the singer

philanderer = man who flirts with women
USE = *

phlegm = coldness or indifference
USE = *

piddling = trivial
USE = we made a piddling profit of Rs 20,000 last year

plagiarist = one who steals words or ideas
USE = *

plait = to braid
USE = a plaited leather belt

plastic = flexible, pliable
USE = sheet of plastic

pluck = to pull strings on musical instrument
USE = He sat on the bed, idly plucking the strings of his guitar

pluralistic = including a variety of groups
USE = A pluralist society

ply = carry on, exercise, to join together
USE = Fishermen in small boats ply their trade up and down the coast

polar = related to the poles of the earth
USE = polar bears

poverty = lacking money or possessions
USE = abject poverty

predator = one that preys on others
USE = lions, wolves and other predators

predictive = relating to prediction
USE = the predictive value of this new method

predisposition = tendency, inclination
USE = an annoying predisposition to find fault

prescient = Foreknowing
USE = a prescient warning

prestidigitation = sleight of hand
USE = *

primeval = ancient, primitive
USE = primeval forests

procrastinator = one who continually and unjustifiably postpones
USE = *

profundity = great depth
USE = the profundity of his remarks

profuse = lavish, extravagant
USE = profuse apologies

proliferation = propagation, reproduction
USE = the proliferation of TV channels

prose = ordinary language used in everyday speech
USE = her prose is lucid

prosecutor = person who initiates a legal action or suit
USE = public prosecutor

protestation = declaration
USE = Ignoring my protestations, they went ahead

pry = to intrude into, force upon
USE = As a reporter, I was paid to pry into other people's lives

pudgy = Small and fat
USE = I was a pudgy child

purgation = process of cleansing
USE = *

quadrilateral = four-sided polygon
USE = Squares and rectangles are quadrilaterals

quaternary = relating to four units or members
USE = *

query = To make inquiry
USE = do you have any queries about your treatment

quiescence = Quiet, inactivity
USE = the political situation is relatively quiescent

raging = violent, wild
USE = a raging temper

raillery = Good-humored satire
USE = *

ramble = walk for pleasure, discuss
USE = Shall we go rambling tomorrow

rarefy = to make thinner, purer, or more refined
USE = *

rational = logical, reasonable
USE = a rational course of action

ravine = deep, narrow gorge
USE = *

raw = vulgar, coarse
USE = *

rebarbative = irritating, repellent
USE = *

rebut = to refute by evidence or argument
USE = She has rebutted charges

recurrence = repetition
USE = a recurrence of symptoms

refract = To bend from a direct course
USE = The glass prism refracted the white light into the colors of the rainbow

refuge = escape, shelter
USE = The climbers slept in a mountain refuge

regard = high esteem
USE = I have high regards for you

remedy = to cure, correct
USE = remedy for headaches

remission = lessening, relaxation
USE = Her cancer has been in remission for several years

remote = distant, isolated
USE = a remote village

renitent = resisting pressure, obstinate
USE = *

repast = meal or mealtime
USE = Yet that simple repast was fit for a king

repentant = apologetic, guilty
USE = he was repentant about his mistakes

reprehend = To find fault with
USE = *

repression = act of restraining or holding in
USE = political repression

restorative = having the power to renew
USE = a restorative and preventive remedy

restrained = controlled
USE = a more restrained policy

retard = to slow
USE = severely retarded economic growth

revitalize = to renew, give new energy to
USE = the new investment has revitalized this part of the country

rhythm = regular pattern or variation of sounds
USE = no sense of rhythm

riddle = to make many holes in, permeate
USE = The anti-aircraft guns riddled the plane's wings with bullets

root = to dig
USE = She rooted through the papers on her desk

rooted = to have an origin or base
USE = deeply-rooted beliefs

rotund = round in shape, fat
USE = *

ruffled = irritated
USE = ruffled by criticism

scabbard = The sheath or cover of a sword
USE = *

scantiness = barely enough, meager
USE = *

scathing = harshly critical, painfully hot
USE = He was very scathing about the report, saying it was inaccurate

score = notation for a musical composition
USE = a film score

scrivener = professional who copies
USE = *

scrutiny = careful observation
USE = the record will come under the scrutiny

secant = Cutting, especially into two parts
USE = *

sepulchral = typical of a place of burial
USE = a gloomy, sepulchral set for the play

signify = denote, indicate
USE = Nobody really knows what the marks on the ancient stones signify

simple = lacking in knowledge or intelligence
USE = He's a bit simple

simulated = fake, made to look real
USE = In cheap furniture, plastic is often used to simulate wood

sincere = genuine, true
USE = a sincere apology

slipshod = careless, hasty
USE = She complained that the carpenter's work had been slipshod

smutty = obscene, indecent
USE = his smutty jokes

solarium = room or glassed-in area exposed to the sun
USE = the solarium on the hill

solidarity = unity based on common aims or interests
USE = to show solidarity with their students

solipsism = belief that the self is the only reality
USE = *

sonic = relating to sound
USE = a supersonic jet plane

Spartan = Exceptionally brave; rigorously severe
USE = Spartan living conditions

speculation = contemplation
USE = he dismissed the rumors as pure speculation

speculative = involving assumption, theoretical
USE = The article was dismissed as highly speculative

splendid = grand, illustrious
USE = splendid food

sprightly = Vivacious, energetic
USE = a sprightly old man

spur = to prod
USE = spurring the economy to faster growth

squabble = To quarrel
USE = having a squabble

stalk = to hunt, pursue
USE = The police had been stalking the woman for a week

stand = group of trees
USE = *

stasis = motionless state, standstill
USE = She was bored - her life was in stasis

steady = stable, unfaltering
USE = I'll hold the boat steady while you climb in

stockade = enclosed area forming defensive wall
USE = *

stripling = A mere youth
USE = *

subdued = suppressed, stifled
USE = subdued lighting

subjection = dependence, obedience, submission
USE = the political subjection of the island by its largest neighbor

subpoena = an order to come to court
USE = They were subpoenaed to testify before the judge

substantial = important, real
USE = a substantial difference

sufferable = bearable
USE = *

suffragist = one who advocates extended voting rights
USE = *

supplicant = One who asks humbly and earnestly
USE = *

surplus = excess
USE = large food surpluses

survey = to examine in a comprehensive way
USE = He got out of the car to survey the damage

sustain = experience, support, nourish
USE = sustain its growth

symbiosis = cooperation, mutual helpfulness
USE = *

syncopation = temporary irregularity in musical rhythm
USE = *

tarnished = corroded, discolored
USE = *

taxonomy = scientific method of classification
USE = *

technocrat = technical expert
USE = With degrees of BE and M Tech, I am a technocrat

teeter = to waver or move unsteadily
USE = she was teetering around in five-inch heels

temperance = being moderate
USE = *

tempered = moderated, restrained
USE = bad-tempered

tinge = to color slightly
USE = tinges of pink

titan = person of colossal stature or achievement
USE = a clash of the titans

tottering = barely standing
USE = She walked slowly with tottering steps

CD 15

abstinence = Self denial
USE = observe abstinence

abusive = using harsh words or ill treatment
USE = abusive father

accelerate = To move faster
USE = accelerate your car

accessible = find, approachable
USE = such information is accessible to the general public

acknowledge = to recognize or accept
USE = acknowledged expert

adorn = to decorate
USE = the room was adorned with flowers

advert = advertisement, refer to
USE = since you advert to this matter frequently, it must be important

affirm = to assert confidently, testify
USE = the speech affirmed government's commitment to education

affluence = abundant supply of money
USE = the child had only seen affluence

agglomeration = collection, heap
USE = agglomeration of miscellaneous items

albeit = although, even if
USE = he tried, albeit without success

alchemy = chemistry of changing base metals to gold in old ages
USE = *

alimony = the money paid by a man to his wife after their divorce
USE = *

alloy = a mixture as of metals
USE = something made of alloy

altruist = One who practices altruism
USE = Gandhi ji was an altruist

ambidextrous = able to use both hands equally well
USE = an ambidextrous painter

amicable = Done in a friendly spirit
USE = an amicable agreement

amnesia = the loss of memory
USE = suffering from amnesia

amputate = To remove by cutting, as a limb
USE = his leg had to be amputated

anemia (BRITISH = anaemia) = Deficiency of blood or red corpuscles
USE = suffering from anemia, he looked pale

anesthetic (BRITISH = anaesthetic) = producing loss of sensation
USE = anesthetic medicine

anonymous = Of unknown authorship
USE = an anonymous letter

antagonism = Mutual opposition
USE = don't take antagonism personally

anthropologist = student of the history and science of human kind
USE = the anthropologist uncovered ancient human remains

anticlimax = change from what was expected
USE = death of the hero in the movie was an anticlimax

antiseptic = Anything that destroys the growth of micro-organisms
USE = antiseptic is used on wounds

apprehend = arrest
USE = police apprehended the thief

appropriate = suitable for a particular situation or person
USE = is this dress appropriate for the party

arrogant = believing one is better than other people
USE = arrogant behavior

asteroid = small planet
USE = *

astigmatism = an eye defect leading to improper focusing
USE = *

atheist = one who does not believe in god
USE = a confirmed atheist

atrocity = Great cruelty or reckless wickedness
USE = Soldiers sometimes commit atrocities against civilians

authentic = real or true
USE = authentic painting

authoritative = authentic, official
USE = an authoritative guide

autopsy = examination of a dead body by dissection
USE = They performed an autopsy

awe = reverential wonder or fear
USE = awe-inspiring, awestruck

babble = to talk foolishly or murmur
USE = he was just babbling

bait = food offered to fish to catch them; anything offered as part of a trap
USE = a mouse trap baited with cheese

beneficiary = One who is lawfully entitled to proceeds of an estate or property
USE = Her husband was the chief beneficiary of her will

bizarre = odd, fantastic
USE = a bizarre incident

bland = boring or without taste
USE = The food was bland

blunder = a mistake
USE = it was a big blunder

braggart = someone who boasts
USE = *

breadth = width
USE = *

bristle = a short, stiff hair or to show annoyance
USE = She bristled at the suggestion that it was her fault

brochure = a pamphlet
USE = a product brochure

bullion = gold and silver in the shape of rods or bars
USE = *

bureaucracy = too many people in an organization
USE = the university's bureaucracy

calligraphy = art of beautiful writing
USE = *

carat = a unit of weight used for gems
USE = a one carat diamond

carnage = massacre
USE = a scene of dreadful carnage.

casualty = serious accident or disaster
USE = The rebels suffered heavy casualties

cataract = Opacity of the lens of the eye resulting in complete or partial blindness
USE = cataract operation

catastrophe = Any great and sudden calamity
USE = natural catastrophe

centigrade = a unit of measuring temperature
USE = *

centrifugal = radiating, departing from the center
USE = centrifugal force

centurion = A captain of one hundred soldiers in the ancient Roman
USE = *

ceremonious = Observant of ritual
USE = ceremonious and polite behavior

chameleon = changeable in appearance
USE = like a chameleon, he assumed the political thinking of every group he met

charisma = a natural power which some people have to influence or attract people
USE = a charismatic leader

chassis = framework and working parts of an automobile
USE = chassis of a car

checkered (BRITISH = chequered) = marked by changes in fortune
USE = a checkered career

choreography = art of dancing
USE = *

cite = To refer to specifically
USE = to cite a case

clamber = to climb somewhere with difficulty, especially using your hands and feet
USE = The children clambered into the boat

cliché = an overused expression
USE = *

clientele = clients
USE = *

coincident = Taking place at the same time
USE = it was just a coincidence

combustible = something that burns easily
USE = combustible liquid

compilation = collection
USE = *

compliance = submission, obedience
USE = the design of school building has to be in compliance with the local building code

component = part
USE = computer components

compromise = agree to something which is not exactly what you want
USE = We need to reach a compromise over this issue

compute = to calculate
USE = Compute the ratio

conceit = Self-flattering opinion
USE = The conceit of that man is incredible

concentric = having a common center
USE = concentric circles

conception = beginning, forming of an idea
USE = at conception of the idea

concession = something that you agree to do or give to someone in order to end an argument
USE = Both sides will have to make concessions

conformity = behave according to normal standards
USE = there is too much conformity in this school

conglomeration = mass of material sticking together
USE = *

connotation = the implication of some term, not the literary meaning
USE = foreigners are usually unaware of the connotations of the words they use

conspiracy = when a group of people secretly plan to do something bad or illegal
USE = a conspiracy to overthrow the government

contaminate = To pollute
USE = contaminated water

contest = to dispute or to compete
USE = the defeated candidate contested the election results

context = relating to a particular thing or event
USE = in the context of

conveyance = transportation
USE = public conveyance

corrosive = causing gradual decay
USE = a highly corrosive acid

cosmic = related to the universe
USE = cosmic rays

counterpart = a person or thing which has the same purpose
USE = the prime minister is to meet his counterpart during the visit

couple = join, unite
USE = *

courier = messenger
USE = courier service

cubicle = small chamber
USE = office cubicles

cursive = Writing in which the letters are joined together
USE = cursive writing

deadlock = standstill, stalemate
USE = *

debris = wreckage, ruins, rubbish
USE = *

decelerate = slow down
USE = decelerate vs. accelerate

decomposition = decay
USE = Despite the body's decomposition, the police were able to identify the murdered man

decoy = Anything that allures into danger or temptation
USE = decoys are commonly used for hunting

default = The neglect or omission of a legal requirement
USE = to default on their mortgage repayments

degraded = lowered in rank, debased
USE = the degraded man spoke only of his past glory

demotic = related to the people
USE = a demotic society

detraction = slandering, aspersion
USE = he is offended by your detraction of his ability as a leader

devious = Out of the common or regular track
USE = a devious scheme

diffusion = Dispersion
USE = the process of diffusion in gases

diligence = Careful effort
USE = She hoped that her diligence would be noticed at work

dilute = To make fluid less concentrated by mixing
USE = Dilute the juice with water

discount = disregard
USE = we discounted what he had to say about his old company

discrimination = ability to see differences, prejudice
USE = *

dissection = cutting in pieces
USE = In biology classes at school we used to dissect frogs

distant = reserved or aloof, cold in manner
USE = his distant greeting made me feel unwelcome

eccentricity = Idiosyncrasy
USE = the eccentricity of the genius

ecologist = person who studies the relationship between living things and their environment
USE = the ecologist opposed the new dam

ecstasy = Rapturous excitement or exaltation
USE = they were in ecstasy

effectual = Efficient
USE = a real and effectual understanding

effervesce = To bubble up
USE = *

egoism = to think only about yourself
USE = the actor's egoism

egotism = Self-conceit
USE = the actor's egotism

ejaculation = exclamation
USE = *

elixir = cure-all, something invigorating
USE = *

embed = enclose, place in something
USE = *

empirical = based only on experience, inductive
USE = empirical evidence

energize = invigorate, make forceful and active
USE = *

entrance = put under a spell, carry away with emotion
USE = he was entranced by the stage magician

environ = enclose, surround in medieval days
USE = in old times, Delhi was environed by a wall

equilibrium = A state of balance
USE = the country's economic equilibrium

erotic = related to passionate love
USE = an erotic novel

erudition = Extensive knowledge of
USE = they respected his erudition

espionage = surveillance, observation, reconnaissance
USE = the government developed a system of espionage

esprit de corps = a deep loyalty of members towards the group
USE = the NCC cadets are proud of their esprit de corps

ethnic = racial, tribal
USE = ethnic groups

exchequer = government department in charge of the revenues
USE = *

exertion = effort, expenditure of much physical work
USE = the exertion spent in unscrewing the rusty bolt left her exhausted

extradition = transfer of an accused from one country to another
USE = an extradition treaty

faculty = mental or bodily powers, teaching staff
USE = mental faculties

fancied = imagined, unreal
USE = fancied insults

fanciful = whimsical, visionary
USE = this is a fanciful scheme because it does not consider the facts

fantastic = unreal, grotesque, whimsical
USE = your fears are fantastic because the moon will not fall on the earth

farce = broad comedy, mockery
USE = the interview degenerated into a farce

finite = limited
USE = a finite amount of time

flourish = grow well, prosper, make sweeping gestures
USE = the orange trees flourished in the sun

fluctuation = Frequent irregular change back and forth
USE = fluctuations in share prices

fluency = smoothness of speech
USE = you speak English with fluency and ease

foolhardy = rash
USE = don't be foolhardy, better take advise of the experts

formality = adherence to established rules or procedures
USE = signing this letter is just a formality

formidable = Difficult to accomplish
USE = a formidable task

franchise = privilege, commercial franchise
USE = the city issued a franchise to the company

friction = clash in opinion, rubbing against
USE = let us try to avoid friction in our group

frigid = Lacking warmth
USE = a frigid environment

frustrate = thwart, defeat
USE = we must frustrate their plan to take over the company

functionary = An official
USE = a government functionary

gait = manner of walking
USE = He walked with a slow stiff gait

gaudy = excessively bright, vulgarly showy
USE = her gaudy taste in clothes appalled us

generality = most
USE = the generality of young people

giddy = dizzy
USE = feeling giddy

glaze = to polish, burnish, glimmer, gloss
USE = glazed tiles

glossary = brief explanation of words used in the text
USE = see this word in the glossary

glossy = smooth and shining
USE = a glossy surface

gourmet = an epicure, a person with very fine taste of food
USE = gourmet restaurant

graphic = related to the art of delineating, vividly described
USE = graphic design

gratify = To please, or satisfy a desire or need
USE = He was gratified to see how well his students had done

grotesque = strange and unpleasant
USE = grotesque figures.

grueling (BRITISH = gruelling) = severe, tough, arduous
USE = grueling work

haphazard = random, accidental, arbitrary
USE = haphazard manner

hazardous = dangerous
USE = hazardous situation

hazy = slightly obscure
USE = hazy details

hierarchy = divided into ranks
USE = it was a strict hierarchy

hieroglyphics = picture writing
USE = *

hindrance = An obstacle
USE = I've never considered my disability a hindrance

hoax = a trick, practical joke
USE = he was embarrassed by the hoax

horticulture = the art of gardening
USE = *

hover = hang about, wait nearby
USE = the helicopter hovered over the helipad

hue and cry = outcry
USE = *

hurtle = to dash, to hurl
USE = the runaway train hurtled towards disaster

icon = An image or likeness
USE = Film heroes and heroines are icons for many young people

idiom = A use of words peculiar to a particular language
USE = To "have bitten off more than you can chew" is an idiom

illusion = An unreal image
USE = an optical illusion

illusive = Deceptive
USE = Their hopes of a peaceful solution turned out to be illusory

implication = that which is implied or suggested
USE = implications of your remark

imply = to communicate indirectly
USE = Are you implying that I'm fat?

inarticulate = unable to express clearly
USE = His speech was inarticulate

incidence = Casual occurrence
USE = what a coincidence-both of us are in this hotel

incompatible = unable to exist or work because of basic differences:

USE = we were incompatible as partners

incredulity = a tendency to disbelief
USE = a sense of incredulity, anger and pain

incur = bring upon oneself
USE = to incur debts

indignity = a loss of respect
USE = They were subjected to various indignities

indulgent = Yielding to the desires of oneself
USE = indulgent relative

inference = resulting conclusion
USE = what is the inference

inflate = enhance, heighten, raise, intensify
USE = his claims about the new products were inflated

innovation = change, introduction of something new
USE = she loved innovations just because they were new

insomnia = Sleeplessness
USE = he suffered from insomnia

intellect = the ability to understand and think in an intelligent way
USE = Her energy and intellect are respected all over the world.

interim = Time between acts or periods, temporary
USE = an interim solution

intimidate = To frighten or threaten
USE = he used to intimidate all the kids

intrude = To go unwanted to a place
USE = I hope I'm not intruding.

intuition = Instinctive knowledge or feeling
USE = base your judgment on intuition

invert = To turn upside down
USE = invert the dish

invulnerable = impossible to damage
USE = The command bunker is invulnerable, even to a nuclear attack

irrepressible = full of energy and enthusiasm
USE = Even the rain failed to dampen his irrepressible spirits

iterate = repeat, reiterate
USE = I will iterate the warning

jovial = Merry
USE = He seemed a very jovial chap

jubilation = Exultation
USE = There was jubilation in the crowd as the winning goal was scored

kiosk = a small stall for the sale of newspapers etc
USE = he bought a newspaper at the kiosk

CD 16

lagoon = a small lake, pond, basin
USE = we swam in the lagoon

lateral thinking = thinking which seeks new ways of looking at a problem
USE = Edward DeBono popularized the term "lateral thinking"

leeway = room to move, margin
USE = when you set a deadline, allow a little leeway

leniency = Forbearance
USE = The defending lawyer asked for leniency on the grounds of her client's youth.

lethal = deadly, fatal
USE = lethal weapons

lewd = sexual in an obvious and rude way
USE = a lewd suggestion

lexicographer = One who writes dictionaries
USE = *

libido = sexual impulse
USE = suppression of the libido

lieu = stead
USE = in lieu of

linguistic = related to language
USE = linguistic abilities

longevity = prolonged life
USE = To what do you attribute your longevity

lustrous = Shining
USE = long lustrous hair

mammal = vertebrate animal whose female suckles to its young
USE = humans are mammals

manipulate = operate with the hands, control or change by artful means
USE = he manipulated the results

mediate = negotiate as an agent between parties
USE = mediate between the two sides

meditation = to pay attention to one thing or religious reasons or relaxation
USE = prayer and meditation

merciful = Disposed to pity and forgive
USE = a merciful ruler

mesmerize = To hypnotize
USE = I was completely mesmerized by the performance

metallurgical = related to the art of removing metals from ores
USE = *

metaphysical = Philosophical
USE = metaphysical questions

metropolis = a big city
USE = a sprawling metropolis

migrant = Wandering
USE = migrant workers

mimicry = imitation
USE = she was mimicking the various people in our office

misadventure = An unlucky accident
USE = death by misadventure

miserly = stingy, mean
USE = a miserly person

missile = a flying weapon
USE = a missile launcher

mite = A very small amount
USE = I couldn't eat another mite

mobile = movable, not fixed
USE = mobile phone

mode = prevailing style
USE = mode of payment

modulation = toning down, changing from one key to another
USE = modulation of voice

molecule = the smallest particle of a substance
USE = a water molecule

momentum = An impetus
USE = give new momentum to their plans

monarchy = Government by a single ruler
USE = *

monetary = Financial
USE = monetary policy

monotheism = belief in one god
USE = *

monumental = massive, colossal
USE = a monumental task

moodiness = fits of depression or gloom
USE = the cause of her moodiness

multilingual = having many languages
USE = most Indians are multilingual

multiplicity = the condition of being manifold or very various
USE = a multiplicity of fashion magazines

nautical = related to ships, or navigation
USE = nautical miles

negation = denial
USE = negation of evidence

negligence = not giving enough care or attention
USE = medical negligence

nostalgia = sentimental longing for past times, reminiscence, recollection
USE = that song filled him with nostalgia

nutrient = nourishing substance
USE = nutrient food

obnoxious = Detestable
USE = he's loud and obnoxious

obsessed = consumed, fixated, gripped
USE = obsessed with career success

obstetrician = a doctor who delivers babies
USE = *

omnipresent = universally present, ubiquitous
USE = *

optician = One who makes eye-glasses
USE = *

optimist = person who looks on the bright side
USE = I am an optimist

optometrist = one who fits glasses to remedy visual defects
USE = *

orientation = act of finding oneself in society
USE = I attended the orientation program on my first day in the college

orthography = correct spelling
USE = *

oust = To eject
USE = The president was ousted in a military coup

palatable = tasteful, agreeable
USE = paying taxes is not palatable

pallet = small, poor bed
USE = straw pallet

parallelism = essential likeness, similarity
USE = there is a striking parallelism between the twins

paranoia = type of a psychological disease where a person thinks everybody hates him
USE = *

passive = Unresponsive
USE = He's very passive in the relationship

pathology = the study of diseases
USE = *

patriarch = the male leader of a family
USE = *

pendant = Anything that hangs from something else
USE = a beautiful necklace with a diamond pendant.

percussion = The sharp striking of one body against another
USE = Drums are percussion instruments

perturb = to worry someone

USE = News of the arrest perturbed her greatly.

perverse = Unreasonable
USE = a perverse logic

perversion = Diversion from the true meaning or proper purpose
USE = His testimony was clearly a perversion of the truth.

pessimism = belief that life is basically bad or evil, gloominess
USE = pessimism vs. optimism

plagiarism = The stealing of writing and publishing as one's own
USE = the editor recognized the plagiarism and returned the manuscript

plausible = Seeming likely to be true, though open to doubt
USE = a plausible explanation

podiatrist = the foot doctor
USE = *

potential = Anything that may be possible
USE = potential buyers

practicable = feasible
USE = not practicable to complete the tunnel soon

predatory = one that eats others
USE = The owl is a predatory bird which kills its prey with its claws

presumption = That which may be logically assumed to be true until disproved
USE = The presumption of innocence is central to Indian law

procrastinate = to delay, postpone, put off
USE = I'm just procrastinating the problem

protrude = To push out or thrust forth
USE = protruding ears

prune = to cut expenditure or branches, trim
USE = she pruned her manuscript into publishable form

psyche = soul, mind
USE = the psyche of people

psychiatrist = a doctor who treats mental diseases
USE = a psychiatrist often spends hours with a patient before making a diagnosis

psychosis = mental disorder
USE = *

pyromaniac = person obsessed with setting fires
USE = *

quietude = tranquility
USE = the monk lived in quietude of the jungle

ramp = slope, inclined plane
USE = ramps are built in hospitals so that people on wheel chairs can move easily

rationalization = bringing into conformity with reason
USE = She rationalized the expense by saying that the costly item would last longer

rebate = discount
USE = a tax rebate

recession = withdrawal, retreat, time of low economic activity
USE = The country was sliding into the depths of recession

recluse = One who lives in retirement or seclusion
USE = He is a millionaire recluse who refuses to give interviews.

recuperate = To recover
USE = recuperating after the operation.

recurrent = Returning at regular or stated intervals
USE = a recurrent nightmare

regeneration = spiritual birth
USE = modern penologists strive for regeneration of the prisoners

reimburse = To pay back an expenditure
USE = the company reimbursed me for the travel expenses

remunerate = To pay
USE = He is remunerated well and he works hard

renovate = To restore after deterioration, as a building
USE = He renovates old houses and sells them

renunciation = An explicit disclaimer of a right or privilege
USE = the renunciation of violence

repository = A place in which goods are stored
USE = libraries are repositories of world's best thoughts

repulsion = act of driving back, distaste
USE = the repulsion of the enemy forces

resignation = patient submissiveness, statement that one is quitting the job
USE = They received the news with resignation

responsiveness = state of reacting readily to appeals, orders, etc
USE = the audience applauded, delighting the singers by its responsiveness

restraint = controlling force
USE = an independent life, free of all restraints

resurgent = Surging back or again
USE = the resurgent militarism in the country.

retraction = withdrawal
USE = he dropped the libel case after the newspaper published a retraction of its statements

reverberate = to echo, resonate, resound
USE = the entire temple reverberated with the sounds of bells

rote = Repetition as a means of learning them
USE = rote learning

rubble = fragments
USE = The bomb reduced the house to rubble

rudimentary = Being in an incomplete stage of development
USE = Some unusual fish have rudimentary legs.

rusticate = banish to the country, dwell in the country
USE = I love the city life and can't understand how people can rusticate in the suburbs

ruthless = pitiless
USE = a dangerous and ruthless murderer

salvage = Any act of saving property
USE = gold coins salvaged from a shipwreck

sarcasm = Cutting and reproachful language
USE = *

satellite = the moon is a satellite of Earth
USE = *

scanty = meager, insufficient
USE = *

scavenger = animal which feeds on dead animals
USE = *

sedate = calm and relaxed
USE = The speed limit in many areas is a sedate 60 kph

senile = a lack of mental ability because of old age
USE = He spent many years caring for his senile mother

septic = putrid, producing putrefaction
USE = *

severity = harshness
USE = *

shackle = thing which hampers movement, bond, chain, handcuff
USE = *

shoddy = sham, not genuine, inferior
USE = shoddy workmanship

similitude = Similarity
USE = *

simulate = Imitate
USE = plastic is often used to simulate wood.

skeptic (BRITISH = sceptic) = One who doubts any statements
USE = *

skimp = provide scantily, live very economically
USE = *

slacken = slow up, loosen
USE = *

sleazy = flimsy, unsubstantial
USE = *

sleeper = something originally of little value or importance
USE = *

sophistication = artificiality, unnaturalness, act of employing sophistry in reasoning
USE = *

spatial = referring to space
USE = *

stalemate = deadlock
USE = the stalemate was finally broken

stellar = related to the stars
USE = a stellar explosion

stereotyped = over simplified, lacking individually, seen as a type
USE = *

subjective = occurring or taking place in the mind
USE = subjective experience

subsidy = direct financial aid by government, etc.
USE = food subsidy

subversion = An overthrow, as from the foundation
USE = He was found guilty of subversion and imprisoned

swindler = cheat
USE = the swindler was jailed

syllogism = logical reasoning where a conclusion is reached from two statements
USE = *

tantrum = attack of uncontrollable bad temper
USE = she threw tantrums

temper = moderate, tone down, or restrain, toughen steel
USE = *

terminate = to put an end to
USE = terminated the contract

tertiary = third
USE = *

thermal = Of or related to heat
USE = thermal conductivity

thrifty = careful about money, economical
USE = Indians are thrifty

torso = trunk of statue with head and limbs missing, human trunk
USE = *

touchy = sensitive, irascible
USE = a touchy issue

toxic = poisonous
USE = toxic waste

tract = pamphlet, a region of indefinite size
USE = *

trajectory = The path described by a projectile moving under given forces
USE = the trajectory of a bullet

tranquility (BRITISH = tranquillity) = Calmness
USE = I love the tranquility of the countryside.

transition = Passage from one place, condition, or action to another
USE = The health-care system is in transition at the moment.

transparent = Easy to see through or understand
USE = transparent Glass

trappings = outward decorations, ornaments
USE = *

traumatic = related to an injury caused by violence
USE = a traumatic experience from his childhood

tremor = An involuntary trembling or shivering
USE = There was a slight tremor in her voice.

tribulations = distress, suffering
USE = trials and tribulations

trilogy = group of three works
USE = *

turmoil = confusion, strife
USE = *

tycoon = a business magnate, baron, big shot, capitalist
USE = *

ultimate = Beyond which there is nothing else
USE = the ultimate luxury car

unearth = dig up
USE = *

unerringly = infallibly
USE = *

unfaltering = steadfast
USE = *

uninhibited = unrepressed
USE = *

unique = Being the only one of its kind
USE = a unique city

unruly = wild, with no discipline, defiant, indomitable
USE = an unruly crowd

vagabond = A wanderer
USE = They live a vagabond life

valedictory = relating to saying goodbye
USE = a valedictory speech

vampire = ghostly being that sucks the blood of the living beings
USE = *

vegetate = To live in a monotonous, passive way without exercise of the mental faculties
USE = children spend too much time vegetating in front of the TV.

velocity = Rapid motion
USE = high velocity

vendor = A seller
USE = a street vendor

ventriloquist = person who can make his voice appear to come from a different source
USE = *

verbalize = put into words
USE = *

verbiage = Use of many words without necessity
USE = verbiage explanation

verge = border, edge
USE = you are on the verge of a big success

vigilance = watchfulness in guarding against danger
USE = the vigilance of a neighbor

virtual = Being in essence or effect, but not in form or appearance
USE = virtual shopping

visionary = produced by imagination, fanciful, mystical
USE = he was a great visionary

wizardry = sorcery, magic
USE = *

worldly = engrossed in matters of this earth, not spiritual
USE = worldly possessions

zany = absurd, preposterous, mad, crazy
USE = *

CD 17

a la carte = priced separately
USE = from the à la carte menu

a priori = reasoning based on general principles
USE = a priori reasoning

abacus = counting device
USE = abacus was used for counting

abandon = desert, forsake
USE = The match was abandoned because of rain

abdomen = belly
USE = abdominal pain

abduct = kidnap
USE = abducted from his car

abide = submit, endure
USE = He abided in the jungle for forty days

abreast = side-by-side
USE = The motorcyclist came abreast of her car

abroad = overseas
USE = going abroad for studies

abrupt = sudden, unexpected
USE = the actor stopped abruptly

abstain = to refrain deliberately from something
USE = to abstain from alcohol

academy = school
USE = academy of arts

accentuate = emphasize
USE = Her dress was tightly belted, accentuating the slimness of her waist

acclaim = recognition, fame, praise
USE = an acclaimed author

accommodate = adapt
USE = we accommodated the needs of physically challenged

accredit = authorize
USE = accredited organization

accumulate = amass
USE = accumulate wealth

adaptable = pliable
USE = adaptable to change

adjacent = next to
USE = an adjacent building

adjourn = discontinue
USE = meeting was adjourned

administer = manage
USE = The country was administered by the British

admissible = allowable
USE = the new evidence was admissible

adversary = opponent
USE = main adversary

advise = give counsel
USE = His doctor advised him against smoking

aerobics = exercise
USE = She does aerobics

affiliate = associate
USE = my school is affiliated to CBSE

affluent = abundant, wealthy
USE = affluent neighborhood

aftermath = consequence
USE = in the aftermath of the explosion

aggravate = worsen
USE = his comments aggravated the problem

aggressor = attacker
USE = *

aggrieve = to afflict, distress, mistreat
USE = one aggrieved customer complained

aggrieved = unjustly injured
USE = He felt aggrieved at not being chosen for the team

agile = nimble, well coordinated
USE = agile child

agronomy = science of crop production
USE = *

air = discuss, broadcast
USE = game was aired live

alibi = excuse
USE = an alibi for its own failure

allot = allocate
USE = allotted seats on the front rowhint

almanac = calendar with additional information
USE = a farmer's almanac

alms = charity
USE = give alms

altitude = height
USE = flying at an altitude of 10 000 meters

altruism = benevolence, generosity, unselfish concern for other's welfare
USE = an act of altruism

amid = among
USE = amid mounds of books

amphibious = able to operate in water and land
USE = frogs are amphibious

amuse = entertain
USE = Apparently these stories are meant to amuse

annex = to attach
USE = turn left to go to the annex

antagonize = harass
USE = I've no wish to antagonize him

anthrax = disease
USE = anthrax virus

apartheid = racial segregation
USE = the long-awaited dismantling of apartheid in South Africa

apt = suitable
USE = an apt comment

aristocrat = nobleman
USE = an aristocratic family

assassin = murderer
USE = She hired an assassin to kill her rival

atomize (BRITISH = atomise) = vaporize
USE = *

attire = dress
USE = appropriate attire for a wedding

audition = tryout
USE = The film director is holding auditions for a hero

aura = atmosphere, emanation
USE = an aura of mystery

authorize = grant, sanction
USE = Who authorized this expenditure?

avail = assistance
USE = Employees should avail themselves of the opportunity

avant garde = vanguard
USE = avant-garde art

barbarian = savage
USE = The walled city was attacked by barbarian hordes

battery = physical attack
USE = assault and battery

becoming = proper
USE = That's a most becoming dress

befit = to be suitable
USE = it befits for her to be the CEO

beget = produce, procreate
USE = poverty begets hunger, and hunger begets crime

bereave = rob
USE = bereaved parents

biodegradable = naturally decaying
USE = Biodegradable packaging helps reduce pollution

biopsy = removing, tissue for examination
USE = a tissue biopsy

blasphemy = insulting God
USE = to be accused of blasphemy

bliss = happiness
USE = my idea of sheer bliss

bona fide = made in good faith
USE = a bona fide resident

booty = loot
USE = to divide the booty

boycott = abstain in protest
USE = to boycott the meeting

brink = edge
USE = to the brink of failure

brook = tolerate
USE = She won't brook any criticism of her work

cabaret = night club
USE = a cabaret act.

cadet = a student of a military academy
USE = NCC cadets

calculating = scheming
USE = a very cold and calculating character

capital = most significant, pertaining to wealth
USE = capital gain tax

captivate = engross, fascinate
USE = she captivated audiences

cashmere = fine wool from Asia
USE = cashmere wool comes from Kashmir

catastrophic = disastrous
USE = catastrophic result

ceramics = pottery
USE = made of ceramics

chronicle = a history
USE = a chronicle of the Independence Movement

chronology = arrangement by time
USE = the chronology of events

circumcise = remove the foreskin
USE = he was circumcised when 6 years of age

citation = summons to appear in court
USE = The court issued a contempt citation against city council

clan = extended family
USE = the whole clan came to visit us

clone = duplicate
USE = Dolly was the first sheep clone

clout = influence
USE = the Indian maharajas have no real political clout

combine = unite, blend
USE = combined with

commodity = product
USE = commodities market

communion = fellowship
USE = a spiritual communion

compassion = kindness
USE = show a little compassion

competence = skillfulness
USE = You'll soon reach a reasonable level of competence in English

compile = collect
USE = compiling some facts and figures

comprise = To consist of
USE = an orchestra is comprised of musicians

compulsory = obligatory
USE = Wearing seat belts in cars is compulsory by law

concerted = done together
USE = take concerted action

concourse = throng
USE = There's a ticket machine in the main concourse

conducive = helping
USE = noise is not conducive to a good night's sleep

confer = To bestow
USE = An honorary doctorate was conferred on him

conference = meeting
USE = a conference on women's rights

confide = trust another (with secrets)
USE = Did you confide this to any friend

confront = challenge
USE = It's an issue we'll have to confront at some point

confuse = perplex
USE = Stop confusing the issue

consecutive = one after another
USE = the third consecutive weekend

considered = well thought out, contemplated
USE = It is my considered opinion

consortium = cartel
USE = a consortium of computer manufacturers

conspicuous = obvious
USE = He tried not to look conspicuous

conspire = plot
USE = He felt that his colleagues were conspiring together to remove him from his job.

constellation = arrangement of stars
USE = a constellation of film stars

contemplate = meditate
USE = I'm contemplating going abroad for a year

contented = satisfied
USE = a contented smile

contraction = shrinkage
USE = Cold causes contraction of the metal

contractual = related to a contract
USE = under a contractual obligation

contrast = difference, comparison
USE = a marked contrast between

controversial = subject to dispute
USE = a controversial issue

convey = communicate
USE = You don't want to convey the impression that we're not interested

convocation = gathering
USE = a university convocation

counterstrike = strike back
USE = *

court-martial = military trial
USE = he had to face a court-martial for disobeying the commanding officer

crave = desire
USE = Many young children crave attention

critique = examination, criticism
USE = a critique of the new policy

culminate = climax
USE = Their many years of research have finally culminated in a cure for the disease

curriculum = course of study
USE = the school curriculum

cyclone = storm
USE = *

czar = Russian emperor
USE = the Russian czar

de facto = actual
USE = de facto standard

deceive = trick
USE = the company deceived customers

decline = decrease in number
USE = The actor's popularity has declined

decree = official order
USE = military decree

deduce = conclude
USE = *

deduct = subtract
USE = deduct the amount and pay me the rest

deem = judge
USE = deemed university

deficit = shortage
USE = a budget deficit

deflower = despoil
USE = *

defraud = swindle
USE = The company was accused of defrauding its customers.hint

degrade = demean
USE = don't degrade woman

dehydrate = dry out
USE = feeling dehydrated

deity = a god
USE = worship deity

delinquent = negligent, culpable
USE = juvenile delinquents

demoralize = dishearten
USE = completely demoralized team

denote = signify, stand for
USE = The color red is used to denote passion or danger

depart = leave
USE = the train departs from Platform 1

deportment = behavior
USE = speech and deportment lessons

deprive = take away
USE = deprived of sleep

designate = appoint
USE = he was designated as the team captain

detain = confine
USE = A suspect was detained by the police

detract = lessen
USE = All that make-up she wears actually detracts from her beauty, I think

devastate = lay waste
USE = the city was devastated by the bombs

devise = plan
USE = devised a game plan

dictate = command
USE = the dictates of conscience

diligent = hard-working
USE = diligent about his work

discord = lack of harmony
USE = religious discord

discourse = conversation
USE = a discourse on the nature of life after death

discreet = prudent
USE = please, be discreet about it

discriminating = able to see differences
USE = discriminating shoppers

disengage = release, detach
USE = He gently disengaged his hand from hers.

disfigure = mar, ruin
USE = he was horribly disfigured by burns

dismal = gloomy
USE = a dismal performance

dismay = dread
USE = filled with dismay

dispatch = send
USE = to dispatch the letters

dispossess = take away possessions
USE = dispossessed of their homes

dissolution = disintegration
USE = the assembly was dissolved

distract = divert
USE = Don't distract her from her studies

dividend = distributed profits
USE = Dividends are sent to shareholders

dock = curtail
USE = The University has docked lecturers' pay by 20% because of their refusal to mark examination papers

don = assume, put on
USE = He donned his finest suit

double-entendre = having two meanings one of which is sexually suggestive
USE = he entertained us with double-entendre

doughty = resolute, unafraid
USE = *

draconian = harsh
USE = draconian laws

duet = twosome
USE = a duet song

ejaculate = exclaim
USE = You've got my umbrella! he ejaculated

elate = raise spirits
USE = you will feel elated on your success

electorate = voters
USE = the wishes of the electorate

elegant = refined, exquisite
USE = a very elegant suit

elite = upper-class
USE = the country's educated elite

eloquent = well-spoken
USE = an eloquent speaker

elude = evade
USE = the solution eluded them

embargo = restriction
USE = America imposed embargo on Iraq

embody = personify
USE = She embodied good sportsmanship on the playing field.

embrace = accept
USE = This was an opportunity that he would embrace

emissary = messenger
USE = the personal emissary of the Prime Minister

employ = use
USE = statistical analysis was employed to obtain these results

empower = enable, grant
USE = we empowered the employees to better help customers

enact = decree, ordain
USE = the government enacted a new law

encapsulate = condense
USE = to encapsulate the story

encyclopedia (BRITISH = encyclopaedia) = A work containing information on subjects, or exhaustive of one subject
USE = the Encyclopedia Britannica

encyclopedic (BRITISH = encyclopaedic) = comprehensive
USE = encyclopedic knowledge

endeavor (BRITISH = endeavour) = attempt, strive
USE = Engineers are endeavoring to locate the source of the problem

endocrinologist = one who studies glands of internal secretion
USE = *

endowment = property, gift
USE = The school has received an endowment of a million rupees to buy new books for the library

endure = suffer
USE = We had to endure a nine-hour delay at the airport

enfranchise = liberate
USE = *

engaging = enchanting, charming
USE = an engaging smile

engulf = overwhelm
USE = The flames rapidly engulfed the house

enlighten = inform
USE = Swami Vivekananda became enlightened

enlist = join
USE = enlist the support of local politicians

enterprise = undertaking
USE = a commercial enterprise

entourage = assemblage
USE = entourage of dancers

enviable = desirable
USE = in the enviable position

envision = imagine
USE = When do you envision finishing the project

envoy = messenger
USE = a United Nations special envoy

epic = majestic
USE = a talk of epic proportions

epidemic = spreading rapidly
USE = a flu epidemic

CD 18

episode = incident
USE = an episode of a TV serial

era = period of time
USE = the Gandhi era

err = mistake, misjudge
USE = He erred in agreeing to her appointment

erupt = burst forth
USE = the volcano erupted

eternal = endless
USE = eternal arguing

etiquette = manners
USE = social etiquette

evangelical = proselytizing
USE = the Evangelical movement

eventful = momentous
USE = an eventful journey

evolution = gradual change
USE = Darwin's theory of evolution

exact = use authority to force payment
USE = The blackmailers exacted a total of a million rupees from their victims

exacting = demanding, difficult
USE = an exacting training schedule

exclaim = shout
USE = Rubbish! he exclaimed in disgust

exclude = shut out
USE = are excluded from the club

exclusive = prohibitive
USE = an exclusive interview

exempt = excuse
USE = exempted from the tax increase

exhaustive = thorough
USE = an exhaustive study

exhibitionist = one who draws attention to himself
USE = he is an exhibitionist on the dance floor

exile = banish
USE = The king went into exile

expanse = extent of land
USE = the immense expanse of the sea

expel = drive out
USE = The new government has expelled all foreign diplomats

expose = divulge
USE = a searing exposé of police corruption

extemporize = improvise
USE = I'd lost my notes and had to extemporize

extent = scope
USE = the extent of his injuries

extract = to pull out, exact
USE = The tooth was eventually extracted

extradite = deport, deliver
USE = He will be extradited to India from Britain

fabrication = a lie
USE = The evidence he gave in court was a complete fabrication

fallacy = false belief
USE = it's a fallacy that problems disappear if you ignore them.

fatal = resulting in death
USE = the fatal shooting

feat = deed
USE = The Eiffel Tower is a remarkable feat of engineering

fertile = fruitful
USE = fertile land

font = source, fountainhead, set of type
USE = *

forthright = frank
USE = a forthright reply

fragile = Easily broken
USE = fragile crockery

fragmented = broken into fragments
USE = increasingly fragmented society

fraternity = brotherhood
USE = a means of promoting fraternity

fruitful = productive
USE = a most fruitful discussion

fuming = angry
USE = fuming at the injustice

gainful = profitable
USE = in search of gainful employment

genetics = study of heredity
USE = *

gingivitis = inflammation of the gums
USE = *

gracious = kindness
USE = a gracious smile

gradient = incline, rising by degrees
USE = a steep gradient

gradual = by degrees
USE = a gradual improvement

gratitude = thankfulness
USE = to show her gratitude

habituate = accustom
USE = *

havoc = destruction
USE = The storm wreaked havoc in the garden

heed = follow advice
USE = failing to heed warnings

herald = harbinger
USE = The president's speech heralds a new era in foreign policy

hermit = one who lives in solitude
USE = *

heuristic = teaching device or method
USE = *

heyday = glory days
USE = In their heyday

holograph = written entirely by hand
USE = *

homely = plain
USE = The hotel was homely and comfortable

humanities = languages and literature
USE = more interested in the humanities than the sciences

hyperactive = overactive
USE = Hyperactive children

hypertension = elevated blood pressure
USE = a new drug for hypertension

hypocritical = deceiving , two-faced
USE = Their accusations of corruption are hypocritical - they have been just as corrupt themselves

hypoglycemic (BRITISH = hypoglycaemic) = low blood sugar
USE = As a diabetic she was accustomed to the occasional hypoglycemic attack

immunity = exemption from prosecution
USE = He was granted immunity from prosecution

impartial = not biased
USE = an impartial judgment

impede = hinder
USE = a broken-down car is impeding the flow of traffic

imperceptible = slight, intangible
USE = imperceptible changes

imposition = intrusion
USE = the imposition of the death penalty

in toto = in full, entirely
USE = The available information amounts to very little in toto

inadvisable = not recommended
USE = Weight-lifting is inadvisable if you have a weak heart

inaudible = cannot be heard
USE = The traffic noise made her voice inaudible

inborn = innate
USE = an inborn tendency

incest = sexual activity between family members
USE = a victim of incest

incidental = insignificant, minor
USE = incidental details

incinerate = burn
USE = to incinerate waste

incision = cut
USE = The surgeon made a small incision

incomparable = peerless
USE = incomparable beauty

incompatibility = inability to live in harmony
USE = An incompatibility problem prevents the two pieces of software from being used together

inconsiderate = thoughtless
USE = Our neighbors are very inconsiderate

inconspicuous = not noticeable
USE = At parties, he always stands in a corner and tries to look inconspicuous

incorporate = combine
USE = This aircraft incorporates several new safety features

indecent = offensive
USE = an indecent act

indiscreet = Lacking wise judgment
USE = In an indiscreet moment

industrious = hard-working
USE = an industrious worker

infantry = foot soldiers
USE = heavy infantry unit

inflammatory = incendiary
USE = inflammatory speech

infuse = inspire, instill
USE = Her arrival infused the children with enthusiasm

initiation = induction ceremony
USE = the initiation of divorce proceedings

innovative = new, useful idea
USE = innovative ideas

installment (BRITISH = instalment) = portion
USE = pay each installment on time

instant = at once
USE = instant tea, instant coffee

intangible = Not perceptible to the touch
USE = charisma is an intangible quality

integration = unification
USE = cultural integration

intensive = extreme
USE = an intensive course in English

intercept = prevent
USE = The police intercepted a shipment of fake drugs

interstate = between states
USE = the interstate highway system

intricate = complex
USE = an intricate design

intrigue = plot, mystery
USE = people have been intrigued by

inventive = cleaver, resourceful
USE = He is very inventive

inviolate = sacred
USE = For centuries the tomb lay inviolate

invocation = calling on God
USE = *

irate = angry
USE = irate phone calls

irrational = illogical
USE = It's totally irrational

jest = joke
USE = Would I jest about something so important

jubilant = in high spirits
USE = The fans were jubilant about India's victory

jurisdiction = domain
USE = sales are subject to Mumbai jurisdiction only

justify = excuse, mitigate
USE = I can't really justify taking another day off work

Koran = holy book of Islam
USE = *

lactic = derived from milk
USE = lactic acid

laurels = fame
USE = the laurels must surely go to the director of the play

layman = nonprofessional
USE = in layman's terms

liable = responsible
USE = you will be liable for the loss

lieutenant = one acts in place of another
USE = second lieutenant

litigate = contest
USE = you'll have to litigate to get your rights

logistics = means of supplying troops
USE = the logistics of the whole aid operation

lure = entice
USE = the lure of fame

magisterial = arbitrary, dictatorial
USE = *

magnum opus = masterpiece
USE = the painting is considered to be his magnum opus

maladjusted = disturbed
USE = maladjusted children

malevolence = bad intent, malice
USE = an act of great malevolence

mania = madness
USE = a sudden mania for exercise

manslaughter = killing someone without malice
USE = She was sentenced to five years imprisonment for manslaughter

manuscript = unpublished book
USE = the 400-page manuscript

maternity = motherhood
USE = maternity leave

memoir = autobiography
USE = She has written a memoir

memorabilia = things worth remembering
USE = Cricket memorabilia

memorandum = note
USE = memorandum of understanding

migrate = travel
USE = Many Indians migrate to America

milk = extract
USE = The directors milked the company of several million dollars

mince = chop, moderate
USE = not mince your words

minute = very small
USE = a minute quantity

misappropriation = use dishonestly
USE = He was charged with forgery, embezzlement and misappropriation of union funds

miscarry = abort
USE = Sadly, she miscarried eight weeks into the pregnancy

mnemonics = that which aids the memory
USE = mnemonics help you remember better

mobilize = assemble for action
USE = to mobilize voter support

mobocracy = rule by mob
USE = *

module = unit
USE = The full computer program is made up of several modules

molest = bother
USE = The girl had been molested

morale = spirit, confidence
USE = the team's high morale

morphine = painkilling drug
USE = he took morphine for pain

mosque = a place of worship
USE = he prayed in the mosque

motive = reason
USE = a motive for lying

motto = slogan, saying
USE = Our motto is your service

multitude = throng
USE = a multitude of problems

murmur = mutter, mumble
USE = "I love you", she murmured

mutiny = rebellion
USE = rumors of mutiny among the troops

mythical = fictitious
USE = a mythical hero

narrate = tell, recount
USE = can you narrate the event for us

naturalize = grant citizenship
USE = a naturalized US citizen

negate = cancel
USE = increase in our profits has been negated by

neurotic = disturbed
USE = She's neurotic about her weight

nimble = spry, quick
USE = nimble fingers

nominate = propose
USE = He was nominated for the post of chairman

nominee = candidate
USE = All nominees for Treasurer will be considered

notable = remarkable, noteworthy
USE = a notable achievement

noted = famous
USE = a noted writer

nouveau riche = newly rich
USE = *

nuisance = annoyance
USE = power failure was a real nuisance

nymph = goddess
USE = *

objectivity = impartiality
USE = true objectivity in a critic is impossible

oblige = compel
USE = The law obliges companies to pay decent wages to their employees

observant = watchful
USE = he was very observant

obtain = gain possession
USE = to obtain permission

octogenarian = person in eighties
USE = his grandfather is an octogenarian

ocular = related to the eye, optic, visual
USE = *

officiate = supervise
USE = A priest officiated at the wedding

offset = counterbalance
USE = The extra cost of traveling to work is offset by the lower price of houses here

omnibus = collection, compilation
USE = the omnibus edition

operative = working
USE = The agreement will not become operative until all members have signed

oppress = persecute
USE = oppressed by a ruthless dictator

oppressive = burdensome
USE = an oppressive government

opt = decide, choose
USE = he opted for early retirement

orderly = neat
USE = She put the letters in three orderly piles

otherworldly = spiritual
USE = The children in the picture look delicate and otherworldly

ovation = applause
USE = standing ovation

overrule = disallow
USE = In tennis, the umpire can overrule the line judge

overwhelm = overpower
USE = overwhelmed by grief

pact = agreement
USE = a free-trade pact

pagan = heathen, ungodly
USE = a pagan festival

page = attendant
USE = *

pageant = exhibition, show
USE = a beauty pageant

pains = labor
USE = she was in labor pains

pantry = storeroom
USE = get tea from the office pantry

paranoid = obsessively suspicious, demented
USE = He started feeling paranoid and was convinced his boss was going to fire him

paranormal = supernatural
USE = paranormal powers

parcel = package
USE = a food parcel

parrot = mimic
USE = she just parrots anything that her mom says

partition = division
USE = partition of India in 1947

paternal = Fatherly
USE = paternal grandfather

pathogen = agent causing disease
USE = a dangerous pathogen

pawn = pledge
USE = Of all items pawned, jewelry is the most common

peaked = wan, pale, haggard
USE = looked a bit peaked

peculiar = unusual
USE = a peculiar smell

peculiarity = characteristic
USE = we all have our little peculiarities

peddle = sell
USE = peddle drugs

CD 19

pen = write
USE = he penned the story

per se = in itself
USE = Research shows that it is not divorce per se that harms children, but the continuing conflict between parents.

perceptive = discerning
USE = perceptive insights

perfectionist = purist, precisionist
USE = don't be a perfectionist

perforate = puncture
USE = a perforated eardrum

perish = die
USE = Three hundred people perished in the earthquake

perishable = decomposable
USE = perishable food

permutation = reordering
USE = permutations of the numbers

perpendicular = at right angles
USE = the nearly perpendicular side of the mountain

perpetuate = cause to continue
USE = perpetuate the violence

persecute = harass
USE = Religious minorities were persecuted

persevere = persist, endure
USE = persevere in your efforts for great success

persona = social façade
USE = his public persona

personify = embody, exemplify
USE = In Greek myth, love is personified by the goddess Aphrodite

personnel = employees
USE = military personnel

persuasive = convincing
USE = a persuasive speaker

pertain = to relate
USE = the parts of the proposals that pertain to local issue

peruse = read carefully
USE = He opened a newspaper and began to peruse

pessimist = cynic
USE = Don't be such a pessimist

petite = small
USE = She was dark and petite

petition = request
USE = I signed a petition against

phenomenal = unusual natural events, or extraordinary
USE = a phenomenal success

philanthropic = charitable
USE = a philanthropic society

philatelist = stamp collector
USE = *

philosophical = contemplative
USE = philosophical writings

physique = frame, musculature
USE = a very powerful, muscular physique

piecemeal = one at a time
USE = everything is being done piecemeal

pine = languish
USE = pined away and died

pitiable = miserable, wretched
USE = a pitiable state of affairs

pivotal = crucial
USE = a pivotal role

pleasantry = banter, persiflage
USE = After exchanging pleasantries

plentiful = Abundant
USE = a plentiful supply of

plight = sad situation
USE = the plight of the poor

plutonium = radioactive material
USE = a bomb made of plutonium

polychromatic = many-colored
USE = *

ponder = muse, reflect
USE = to ponder her next move

posthaste (BRITISH = post-haste) = hastily
USE = They traveled posthaste to Rome to collect the award

potent = powerful
USE = a potent drug

preconception = prejudgment, prejudice
USE = without too many preconceptions

predisposed = inclined
USE = genetically predisposed to cancer

prefabricated = ready-built
USE = a prefabricated house

prefect = magistrate
USE = appointed as Prefect

preference = choice
USE = preference is for tea

preferment = promotion
USE = *

preliminary = introductory
USE = Preliminary results

prenatal = before birth
USE = the prenatal clinic

prerequisite = requirement
USE = a prerequisite for success

presentable = acceptable, well-mannered
USE = was looking quite presentable

preside = direct, chair
USE = to preside over the public enquiry

pressing = urgent
USE = a pressing issue

presume = deduce
USE = I presume that they're not coming

presuppose = assume
USE = All this presupposes that he'll get the job he wants

pretense (BRITISH = pretence) = affection, excuse
USE = She made absolutely no pretence of being interested.

prevailing = common, current
USE = the prevailing attitude

prick = puncture
USE = She pricked the balloon with a pin

primal = first, beginning
USE = primal fears

primate = head, master
USE = He was made the Roman Catholic Primate of All Ireland

princely = regal, generous
USE = a princely childhood

problematic = uncertain
USE = problematic situation

procedure = method
USE = correct procedure

proceeds = profit
USE = The proceeds of today's festival will go to local charities

proclaim = announce
USE = All the countries have proclaimed their loyalty to the alliance

procreate = beget
USE = the right to marry and procreate

prodigy = a person with extraordinary ability or talent
USE = a child prodigy

profess = affirm
USE = She professes not to be interested in money

profiteer = extortionist
USE = a war profiteer

profound = deep, knowledgeable
USE = profound wisdom

proliferate = increase rapidly
USE = Coaching institutes have proliferated in the last ten years

prolong = lengthen in time
USE = decided to prolong our stay

prompt = induce
USE = The speech has prompted an angry response

propaganda = publicity
USE = political propaganda

prophet = prognosticator
USE = the words of the prophet

proportionate = commensurate
USE = Weight is proportional to size

proposition = offer, proposal
USE = a business proposition

proprietor = manager, owner
USE = a newspaper proprietor

prospective = expected, imminent
USE = prospective employers

prospectus = brochure
USE = impressive prospectus

proverb = maxim
USE = an old proverb

proverbial = well-known
USE = his proverbial good humor

providence = foresight, divine protection
USE = divine providence

province = bailiwick, district
USE = the province of Rajasthan

provisional = temporary
USE = a provisional certificate

provisory = conditional
USE = *hint

provocative = titillating
USE = a provocative question

psychopath = madman
USE = *

psychotic = demented
USE = a psychotic disorder

puberty = adolescence
USE = At puberty, girls begin to menstruate

pulp = paste, mush
USE = Mash the bananas to a pulp

pulpit = platform, priesthood
USE = the priest spoke from the pulpit

pun = wordplay
USE = a well-known joke based on a pun

purposeful = determined
USE = He has a quiet, purposeful air

pursuant = following, according
USE = pursuant to an order

pygmy = dwarf
USE = a political pygmy

pyrotechnics = fireworks
USE = pyrotechnics show on the Independence Day

quantum = quantity, particle
USE = a quantum leap

quarter = residence
USE = government quarters

questionnaire = interrogation
USE = fill in a questionnaire

quota = a share or proportion
USE = the usual quota

rapidity = speed
USE = *

reap = harvest
USE = reap the benefit

recede = move back
USE = The painful memories gradually receded in her mind

recital = performance
USE = a piano recital

recitation = recital, lesson
USE = recitation of some poem

recoil = flinch, retreat
USE = I recoiled from the smell

recollect = remember
USE = As far as I can recollect

recoup = recover
USE = recouped his losses

recuperation = recovery
USE = he fell from the horse and the recuperation took three months

redoubt = fort
USE = the last redoubt of upper-class privilege

reel = stagger
USE = She hit him so hard that he reeled backwards

refined = purified, cultured
USE = refined oil

refrain = abstain
USE = Please refrain from smoking

regrettable = lamentable
USE = a deeply regrettable mistake

rehash = repeat
USE = His new book is just a rehash

reincarnation = rebirth
USE = Hindus and Buddhists believe in reincarnation

rejoice = celebrate
USE = She rejoiced in her good fortune

relapse = recurrence of illness
USE = relapse of malaria

relentless = unstoppable
USE = relentless criticism

relic = antique
USE = During the dig, the archeological team found some relics from the Stone Age

repatriate = to send back to the native land
USE = The government repatriated him because he had no visa

repulsive = repugnant
USE = I think rats are repulsive

repute = esteem
USE = a place of ill repute

requisition = order
USE = The staff made a requisition for

reside = dwell
USE = My family now resides in India

resigned = accepting of a situation
USE = a resigned look

resilience = ability to recover from an illness
USE = *

resort = recourse
USE = He got back the money legally, without resort to violence

resourceful = inventive, skillful
USE = a resourceful manager

respectively = in order
USE = first and third position respectively

resurgence = revival
USE = resurgence in demand

retainer = advance fee
USE = he paid the lawyer Rs 1,000 as retainer

revamp = recast
USE = We revamped all the management system

revenue = income
USE = revenues fell dramatically

revision = new version
USE = These proposals will need a lot of revision

revive = renew
USE = to revive someone's hopes

rheumatism = inflammation
USE = suffer from rheumatism

rogue = scoundrel
USE = a rogue state

rouse = awaken
USE = He roused himself and got back to work

rudiment = beginning
USE = rudiments of an experiment

sabbatical = vacation
USE = sabbatical leave

sabotage = treason, destruction
USE = attempt to sabotage the ceasefire

sacred cow = idol, taboo
USE = the sacred cow of parliamentary democracy

saddle = encumber, burden, strain
USE = put a saddle on the horse

safari = expedition
USE = to go on safari

sage = wise person
USE = sage advice

salvation = redemption
USE = a marriage beyond salvation

sans = without
USE = *

satanic = pertaining to the Devil
USE = a satanic cult

savvy = perceptive
USE = business savvy

scant = inadequate, meager
USE = scant regard for the truth

scheme = plot
USE = All her ministers were scheming against her

scorn = disdain, reject
USE = She has nothing but scorn for him

scoundrel = unprincipled person
USE = a heartless scoundrel

scruples = misgivings
USE = Robin Hood had no scruples about robbing the rich to give to the poor

scrutinize = examine closely
USE = He scrutinized the men's faces carefully

secure = make safe
USE = Endangered species need to be kept secure from poachers

sedation = state of calm
USE = She's under strong sedation

seduce = lure
USE = I was seduced by the low price

seismic = pertaining to earthquakes
USE = seismic activity

self-effacing = modest
USE = The captain was typically self-effacing, giving credit to the other players

semantics = study of word meanings
USE = semantics describes what words mean

seniority = privilege due to length of service
USE = promotion will be based on seniority

sensational = outstanding
USE = a sensational sports car

sensible = wise
USE = a sensible answer

sensory = relating to senses
USE = sensory appeal

sensualist = epicure
USE = *

serene = peaceful
USE = She has a lovely serene face

session = meeting
USE = The parliamentary session

sever = cut in two
USE = Her foot was severed from her leg in a car accident

shortcomings = deficiencies
USE = Like any political system, it has its shortcomings

signatory = signer
USE = are signatories to

singular = unique
USE = singular grace and beauty

site = location
USE = the site for the new hospital

slate = list of candidates
USE = he is slated to be the next captain of the cricket team

snub = ignore
USE = she felt snubbed

socialite = one who is prominent in society
USE = a wealthy socialite

sociology = study of society
USE = a degree in sociology

solemn = serious, somber
USE = a solemn face

solemnity = seriousness
USE = the solemnity of a funeral service

specimen = sample
USE = a collection of rare insect specimens

speculate = conjecture
USE = to speculate on the cause of train crash

spindle = shaft
USE = *

spirited = lively
USE = high-spirited

spite = malice, grudge
USE = just out of spite

splurge = indulge
USE = I feel like splurging on a new dress

statute = regulation
USE = a new statute on taxes

staunch = loyal
USE = staunch supporter

stealth = secrecy, covertness
USE = These thieves operate with stealth

stenography = shorthand
USE = *

stimulate = excite
USE = stimulate students to think

stipulate = specify, arrange
USE = The law stipulates that

stole = long scarf
USE = a mink stole

striking = impressive, attractive
USE = her striking looks

strive = endeavor
USE = strive to live up to the expectations

submit = yield
USE = We protested about the changes, but in the end we had to submit

subordinate = lower in rank
USE = a subordinate role

subside = diminish
USE = the violence will soon subside

subsidize = financial assistance
USE = to subsidize the training

suffice = adequate
USE = I think that should suffice

suggestive = thought-provoking, risque
USE = The amplified sounds are suggestive of dolphins chatting to each other under the sea

summon = call for, arraign
USE = to summon reinforcements

superb = excellent
USE = a superb performance

superintend = supervise
USE = Her job is to superintend the production process

superlative = superior
USE = a superlative restaurant

Free Bonus Book:
1853 Most Difficult GRE Words

(Word List with Meanings)

Dear Friend,

This is a valuable list of 1,853 most difficult GRE words that can give you an edge over others.

This is my gift to you with my best wishes for your big success in GRE and in life.

Wishing you best of success in GRE for admission to a top college and worldwide opportunities for exciting career, great wealth, enriching travel, and family pride,

Franklin Vocab System Team

amphitheater (BRITISH = amphitheatre) = oval-shaped theater

anathema = curse, ban

annul = cancel, nullify

anodyne = pain soothing

anoint = consecrate, to apply oil, especially as a sacred rite

anonymity = state of being anonymous, having no name

antediluvian = ancient, obsolete, pre historic

antithesis = direct opposite

apathetic = unconcerned, indifferent

aphasia = inability to speak or use words

aphorism = maxim, old saying

aplomb = poise, confidence

apocryphal = a doubtful authenticity, not genuine, fictional

apostate = one who abandons one's faith

apotheosis = Deification, glorification

approbation = praise, official approval

archaic = Antiquated, from an earlier time

archipelago = group of islands

ardor (BRITISH = ardour) = great emotion or passion

arraign = indict, to call to court to answer a charge

arrogate = seize without right, to demand or claim arrogantly

ascendancy = powerful state

ascribe = to attribute

ashen = resembling ashes, or deathly pale

asinine = stupid

askance = to view with suspicion, scornfully

askew = crooked, tilted

aspersion = slander, false rumor, damaging report

assail = attack

assent = to express agreement

assiduous = hard-working, diligent, persistent

assuage = lessen (pain), to make less severe, ease

astringent = causing contraction, severe, harsh

asunder = apart, into different parts

atone = make amends for a wrong

august = noble, dignified, awe-inspiring, venerable

avow = declare

awry = crooked, askew, amiss

axiom = self-evident truth, premise, postulate

bacchanal = orgy, drunkenly festive

baleful = hostile, malignant, harmful with evil intentions

balk = hesitate, refuse, shirk, prevent

banal = trite, overly common

bane = poison, nuisance, something causing ruin

bastion = fort, fortification, stronghold

beguile = deceive, seduce, mislead

behemoth = monster, huge creature

beleaguer = besiege, to harass, plague

berate = to scold harshly

bestial = beast-like, brutal

bestow = to give as a gift, grant

bevy = group

bicker = quarrel, to have a petty argument

bilious = ill-tempered

bilk = swindle, cheat, defraud

blandish = to coax with flattering, grovel

blight = decay, afflict, destroy

blithe = Joyful, cheerful, or without appropriate thought

bombast = pompous speech

bourgeois = middle class

broach = bring up a topic of conversation

brusque = curt, rough and abrupt in manner

bulwark = fortification

burgeon = sprout or flourish

burly = husky, brawny

cabal = plot, a secret group seeking to overturn something

cadaver = corpse, dead body

cajole = encourage, coax, flatter

calumny = Slander, false and malicious accusation

canard = hoax, a lie

candor (BRITISH = candour) = frankness, honesty of expression

canvass = survey, examine thoroughly

capricious = fickle, impulsive, whimsical, without much thought

careen = swerve, to lean on one side

castigate = criticize, punish, chastise

cataclysm = catastrophe, disaster

cathartic = purgative, purifying, cleansing

catholic = universal, worldly

caucus = a small group within an organization or a meeting of such a group

cavil = quibble, raise trivial objections

cede = transfer ownership, to surrender possession of something

censorious = condemning speech, severely critical

chagrin = shame, embarrassment, humiliation

chalice = goblet, cup

chary = cautious, watchful, extremely shy

cherubic = sweet, innocent

chicanery = trickery, fraud, deception

chide = scold, express disapproval

chimerical = imaginary, impossible

choleric = easily angered, short-tempered

circumlocution = roundabout expression

circumspect = cautious, wary

circumvent = evade, avoid, to go around

citadel = fortress or stronghold

clamor (BRITISH = clamour) = noisy outcry

cleave = to split or separate, to stick, adhere

clemency = forgiveness, merciful leniency

cloister = refuge, to confine, seclude

coalesce = combine, to grow together

coddle = to pamper, baby, treat indulgently

cogent = well-put, convincing, logically forceful

cognate = from the same source, related

cognomen = family name, any name, nickname

colloquy = conference

collusion = conspiracy, collaboration, complicity

commodious = spacious

complicity = guilt by association, knowing partnership in wrong doing

compunction = remorse, regret

concur = To agree

conflagration = large fire, big, destructive fire

confluence = flowing together, meeting of two streams, meeting place

confound = bewilder, to baffle, perplex

congeal = solidify, as a liquid freezing, to become thick or solid

conjecture = hypothesis, speculation, prediction

conjure = summon, to evoke a spirit, cast a spell

consanguinity = related by blood, kinship

consecrate = make holy, dedicate to a goal, to declare sacred

construe = interpret or to explain

continence = self-control, self-restraint

contrite = apologetic, deeply sorrowful and repentant for a wrong

contusion = A bruise

conundrum = enigma, puzzle or problem with no solution, riddle

convivial = sociable, festive, fond of eating, drinking, and people

convoke = convene, summon, to call together

coquette = woman who flirts

corroborate = to confirm, verify

coterie = small group, group of people with a common interest or purpose

countenance = facial expression, to favor, support

cower = showing fear, to cringe in fear

crass = crude, unrefined

craven = cowardly

credence = Belief, acceptance of something as true or real

creed = Belief or principle

cringe = cower, to shrink in fear

culpable = blameworthy, guilty, responsible for wrong

cupidity = greed

curmudgeon = boor, cranky person

dally = procrastinate, to act playfully or waste time

debase = to degrade, or lower in quality or stature

debauch = to corrupt, seduce from virtue or duty

debutante = a girl debuting into society

decadence = deterioration, decay (e.g. moral or cultural)

decapitate = kill by beheading

deciduous = shedding leaves, short-lived, temporary

decorous = seemly, proper, tasteful, socially correct

decry = castigate, to belittle, openly condemn

deference = courteously yielding to another, respect, honor

defile = pollute, to make unclean or dishonor

deft = skillful, dexterous

defunct = extinct, no longer existing, dead

deleterious = harmful, destructive, detrimental

deluge = a flood, to submerge, overwhelm

demagogue = An unprincipled politician, leader

demean = to degrade, humiliate, humble

demur = take exception, to express doubts or objections

denigrate = defame, to slur or blacken someone's reputation

depravity = immorality, sinfulness

deprecate = belittle, disparage

deride = To ridicule, to mock, make fun of

desecrate = profane, to abuse something sacred

desiccate = dehydrate, to dry completely

despondent = depressed, feeling discouraged and dejected

desultory = without direction in life, at random, rambling, unmethodical

diatribe = long denunciation, bitter verbal attack

dichotomy = a division into two parts

didactic = instructional

dilettante = amateur, dabbler

disabuse = correct, to free from a misconception

disburse = pay out

disconsolate = inconsolable, unable to be consoled, extremely sad

discrete = separate, distinct

discursive = rambling, wandering from topic to topic

disdain = to regard with scorn and contempt

disingenuous = deceptive, sly and crafty

disjointed = disconnected, incoherent, being separated

disparage = belittle, speak disrespectfully about

disparate = various, dissimilar, different in kind

disparity = difference, contrast, dissimilarity

dispirit = discourage, to dishearten, make dejected

dissipate = scatter

distend = swell, inflate, bloat

distraught = distressed, very worried

docile = domesticated, trained, tame

dotage = senility, mental decline

dour = sullen and gloomy, stern and severe

droll = amusing in a wry

dulcet = melodious, pleasant sounding

duplicity = deceit, treachery, dishonesty, double-dealing

duress = coercion, imprisonment

ebb = recede, to fade away

ebullient = exuberant, full of enthusiasm and high spirits

eclectic = joyful

edify = instruct morally and spiritually

efface = To obliterate

effrontery = insolence

effulgent = brilliant

elicit = provoke

elucidate = make clear, clarify

emaciated = underfed, gaunt

embroil = involve, cause to fall into disorder

emend = correct

encomium = warm praise

encumber = burden, to hinder, restrict motion

endemic = Peculiar to some specified country or people

enervate = weaken, sap strength from

engender = generate, to produce

enigmatic = puzzling, inexplicable

enjoin = urge, order, command

ennui = boredom, lack of interest and energy

enthrall (BRITISH = enthral) = mesmerize, to captivate, enchant

entreat = plead, beg

epicure = gourmet, person with refined taste in food and wine

epigram = saying, short, witty saying or poem

epithet = name, appellation, phrase

equine = pertaining to horses

erode = wear away, to diminish

errant = wandering, mistaken

eschew = avoid, to abstain from

espouse = to support or advocate

estranged = alienated, separated

euthanasia = mercy-killing

evanescent = fleeting, very brief, short-lived

evince = attest, demonstrate, to show clearly

exacerbate = worsen

exasperate = irritate, vex

execrable = very bad, abominable, utterly detestable

exemplary = outstanding, serving as an example

exhort = strongly urge

exhume = uncover, to remove from a grave

exonerate = free from blame

exorcise = to expel evil spirits

expedient = advantageous, convenient, efficient

expiate = atone, make amends for

expunge = erase, eliminate completely

extenuate = To diminish the gravity or importance of

extol = praise highly

extraneous = not essential, unnecessary

extricate = Disentangle, free

exuberant = joyous, happy

exude = emit, ooze

exult = rejoice

facetious = joking, sarcastic, witty

facile = very easy

fallow = unproductive, unplowed

fastidious = meticulous, careful with details

fathom = understand, to measure the depth of

fatuous = inane, stupid

fealty = Loyalty

fecund = fertile, fruitful, productive

feign = pretend, give a false impression

fetid = foul-smelling, putrid, stinking

fickle = always changing one's mind

fidelity = Loyalty

filch = steal something of little value

filial = of a son or daughter

fitful = irregular

flagrant = outrageous, shameless

fledgling = just beginning, struggling

flippant = Having a light, pert, trifling disposition

florid = ruddy, with too much decoration

flout = to show disregard for the law or rules

foible = weakness, minor fault

foist = palm off a fake

foment = instigate

fortuitous = happening by luck, fortunate

foster = encourage

fracas = noisy fight

fraught = filled

frenetic = harried, neurotic

frond = bending tree

fulminate = denounce, menace

fulsome = excessive, insincere

furtive = stealthy

gainsay = to deny

gargantuan = large

garner = gather

garrulous = talkative, loquacious, wordy

gauche = awkward, crude

genre = kind, category

gibe = heckle

glib = insincere manner

glower = stare angrily

goad = encourage

gossamer = thin and flimsy

gouge = overcharge, scoop out

grimace = expression of disgust

grovel = crawl, obey

guile = deceit, trickery

hackneyed = trite

hapless = unlucky

harangue = a pompous speech

harbinger = forerunner

haughty = arrogant

hedonism = the pursuit of pleasure in life

heinous = shocking, wicked

hermetic = airtight, sealed

hew = to cut with an ax

hiatus = interruption

hone = sharpen

illimitable = limitless

imbue = infuse, dye, wet

immure = build a wall around

impair = injure

impassive = calm, without feeling

impeccable = faultless

impecunious = indigent, having no money

imperious = domineering

impertinent = insolent, rude

imperturbable = calm

impervious = Impenetrable

impetuous = quick to act without thinking

implausible = unlikely, inconceivable

impolitic = unwise

importune = urgent request

impregnable = totally safe from attack

impugn = criticize

inadvertent = unintentional

inane = vacuous, stupid

incandescent = brilliant

incarcerate = to put in a jail

incendiary = burning easily, flammable

inchoate = just begun

incipient = beginning to exist

incisive = keen, penetrating

incognito = disguised

incommunicado = unable to communicate with others

incontrovertible = Indisputable

inculcate = instill, indoctrinate, to teach

incumbent = obligatory, required

incursion = raid

indict = charge with a crime

indigenous = Native

indigent = very poor

indolent = lazy

indomitable = invincible, fearless

indubitable = unquestionable

inexorable = relentless, inflexible

infallible = incapable of making a mistake

infernal = hellish

infirmity = ailment, disease

ingrate = ungrateful person

ingratiate = pleasing, flattering, endearing

inimical = adverse, hostile, unfriendly

innocuous = Harmless

innuendo = indirect and subtle criticism

inscrutable = cannot be fully understood

insinuate = to suggest, imply, say indirectly

insipid = flat, dull, lacking flavor

insolent = insulting

insular = narrow-minded, isolated

insuperable = insurmountable

insurgent = rebellious

insurrection = uprising, rebellion

inter = bury

interdict = prohibit

interloper = intruder, meddler in others' affairs

interminable = unending

internecine = mutually destructive

intransigent = uncompromising

intrepid = fearless

inundate = flood

invective = verbal insult

inveigh = to rail against, protest strongly

inveterate = habitual, chronic, long-standing

invidious = incurring ill-will

irascible = irritable

itinerant = Wandering, unsettled

jaded = spent, bored with one's situation

juggernaut = unstoppable force

kismet = fate

knell = sound of a funeral bell

lachrymose = tearful

lampoon = satirize, to attack with satire

larceny = theft of property

largess = generous donation

legerdemain = trickery

levity = Frivolity, humor

libertine = one without moral restraint

licentious = lewd, immoral

limpid = transparent, clearly understood

lissome (BRITISH = lissom) = agile, supple

lithe = moving and bending with ease

loathe = abhor, hate

loquacious = Talkative

lugubrious = sad, sorrowful

lurid = glowing, shocking

macabre = gruesome

machination = plot or scheme

maelstrom = whirlpool, agitated state of mind

malapropism = comical misuse of a word

malcontent = one who is forever dissatisfied

malediction = curse

malefactor = evildoer, culprit

malodorous = fetid, foul-smelling

manifold = multiple, diverse

martial = warlike, pertaining to the military

martinet = strict disciplinarian

masochist = one who enjoys pain

maudlin = weepy, sentimental

maverick = a person who resists adherence to a group

mawkish = sickeningly sentimental

meander = to wander aimlessly without direction

mendicant = beggar

mercurial = changeable, volatile, quick

mettle = courage, capacity for bravery

minatory = threatening

mirth = jollity, laughter

miscreant = one who behaves criminally

missive = letter or note

modicum = a small amount

mollify = to calm or make less severe

moot = disputable, previously decided

mordant = biting, sarcastic

mores = moral standards, customs

moribund = near death

mote = speck, small particle

motley = diverse, many colored

multifarious = diverse, many-sided

munificent = generous

myriad = innumerable

nascent = incipient, coming into existence

natal = related to birth

necromancy = sorcery, black magic

Nemesis = implacable foe, often victorious opponent

neologism = new word or expression

neophyte = beginner

nether = located under or below

nettle = irritate

niggardly = stingy

noisome = harmful, stinking

nonentity = person of no significance

obdurate = unyielding

obeisance = homage, deference

obfuscate = bewilder, muddle, to confuse

oblique = indirect

obliterate = destroy

obloquy = slander, abusive language

obsequious = fawning, servile, overly submissive

obsequy = funeral ceremony

obstinate = stubborn

obstreperous = noisy, unruly, troublesome

obtuse = stupid, dull

occlude = block, to shut

odious = despicable, hateful

onerous = burdensome

opprobrious = abusive, disgraceful

ordain = appoint

ossify = harden

ostensible = apparent, seeming

ostentatious = pretentious, showy

overweening = arrogant, forward

pacifist = one who opposes all violence

paean = a song of praise

palaver = babble, nonsense

pall = to become dull or weary

palliate = to make less serious, ease

pallid = pale, sallow, lacking color or liveliness

palpable = touchable, obvious, real

paltry = scarce, pitifully small or worthless

panache = flamboyance, flair

pandemic = spread over a whole area or country

panegyric = praise

panoply = full suit of armor

paragon = model of excellence or perfection

pariah = outcast

parley = conference, discussion

parry = avert, ward off, reflect

partisan = supporter

pathos = emotion, feeling of sadness

patrician = aristocrat

patrimony = inheritance or heritage derived from one's father

peccadillo = a minor fault

pedagogue = dull, formal teacher

pedant = a person who is too interested in formal rules and small unimportant details

pejorative = insulting, having bad connotations

pellucid = transparent, easily understood

penance = voluntary suffering to repent for a wrong

penchant = inclination

penitent = repentant

pensive = sad

perdition = damnation, complete ruin

peremptory = dictatorial

perennial = enduring, lasting

perfidious = treacherous (of a person)

perfunctory = careless, done in a routine way

peripatetic = moving from place to place

pernicious = destructive

pert = flippant, bold

pertinacious = persevering

pertinent = Relevant, applicable

philistine = barbarian, narrow-minded person

phlegmatic = sluggish, someone who is calm

pillory = punish by ridicule

pique = sting, arouse interest

pithy = concise, to the point

pittance = alms, trifle

placid = Serene, calm

platitude = trite remark, stale

plebeian = common, vulgar

plethora = overabundance

poignant = pungent, sharp, emotionally moving

polemic = a controversy

portend = omen

portly = large, dignified

potentate = sovereign, king

prattle = chatter, foolish talk

precept = principle, law

precipice = cliff, edge

precipitous = steep

precocious = advanced

precursor = forerunner

predilection = inclination, preference

premeditate = plan in advance

preponderance = predominance

preposterous = ridiculous, illogical

presage = omen, indicate in advance

privation = lack of usual necessities or comforts

probity = integrity, complete honesty

proclivity = inclination, tendency

prodigal = wasteful

prodigious = marvelous, enormous

profligate = licentious, prodigal, corrupt

progenitor = ancestor

progeny = children

prognosis = forecast

prognosticate = foretell

prolix = long-winded, wordy

promontory = headland, cape

promulgate = publish, disseminate

propensity = inclination

propinquity = nearness, kinship

propitiate = satisfy, to win over

propitious = auspicious, favorable

prosaic = uninspired, flat, dull

proscribe = prohibit, to condemn

proselytize (BRITISH = proselytise) = recruit, convert

protean = changing readily

protract = To prolong, extend

provident = having foresight, thrifty

prude = puritan

prudent = cautious, careful

prurient = exhibiting lewd desires

puerile = Childish

pugnacious = combative, quarrelsome

pulchritude = beauty

punctilious = careful in observing rules of behavior or ceremony

pungent = sharp smell or taste

purport = claim to be

pusillanimous = cowardly

quaff = to drink heartily

quagmire = difficult situation

quandary = dilemma, difficulty

quell = suppress, allay

querulous = complaining

quibble = to argue about insignificant and irrelevant details

quiescent = still, motionless, at rest

Quixotic = impractical, romantic

raconteur = story teller

rampant = unbridled, raging

rancor (BRITISH = rancour) = resentment, dislike

rant = rage, scold

rapacious = grasping, avaricious, greedy

rapprochement = reconciliation

raze = destroy

recalcitrant = resisting authority or control

recant = retract a statement

recidivism = habitual criminal activity

recondite = known to only a few

recreant = coward, betrayer of faith

refractory = obstinate

regal = royal

relegate = assign to an inferior position

renege = break a promise

replete = complete

reprehensible = blameworthy, unacceptable

reproach = blame

reprobate = morally unprincipled person

reprove = to criticize or correct

repudiate = to reject as having no authority

requiem = rest, a mass for the dead

requite = to return in kind

rescind = revoke, cancel

respite = interval or relief

resplendent = shining, splendid

restitution = act of compensating for loss or damage

restive = nervous, uneasy

retort = quick replay

retrench = reorganize, to regroup

retrieve = reclaim

retrograde = regress

revelry = merrymaking

revere = honor

revile = to criticize with harsh language

revulsion = aversion

ribald = coarse, vulgar

rife = widespread, abundant

risque = off-color, racy

rostrum = stage for public speaking

ruminate = reflect upon

rustic = rural

sacrosanct = sacred

sagacious = wise

sallow = sickly yellow in color

sanguine = cheerful

sapient = wise, shrewd

sardonic = scornful

saunter = walk in a leisurely manner

savant = scholar

schism = a division or separation

scintilla = very small amount

scintillate = sparkle

scoff = ridicule

scurrilous = abusive, insulting

secular = worldly, nonreligious

sedition = treason, resistance to authority

sententious = concise, trying to appear wise

sequester = to remove or set apart

seraphic = angelic, pure

serendipity = making fortunate discoveries

servile = slavish, obedient

simian = monkey like

simper = smile foolishly, smirk

sinecure = well paid position with little responsibility

skulk = sneak about

slake = to calm down or moderate

sloth = laziness

slovenly = sloppy

sobriety = composed

sobriquet = nickname

sodden = soaked

sojourn = trip, visit

solace = consolation

solecism = ungrammatical construction

solicitous = considerate, concerned

soliloquy = A monologue

solstice = furthest point

somber (BRITISH = sombre) = Gloomy

somnambulist = sleepwalker

somnolent = Sleepy

soporific = sleep inducing

sordid = foul, ignoble, dirty and unpleasant

spawn = produce

specious = false but plausible

sporadic = occurring irregularly

sportive = playful

spurn = reject

squalid = filthy

staid = demure, sedate, boring

steadfast = loyal, immovable

stentorian = extremely loud

stigma = mark of disgrace

stilted = formal, stiff, unnatural

stoic = indifferent to pain or pleasure

stolid = impassive

stratagem = trick

stricture = negative criticism

stultify = inhibit, enfeeble

stymie = hinder, thwart

suave = smooth

sublimate = to repress impulses

sublime = lofty, excellent

subterfuge = cunning, ruse

succulent = juicy, delicious

sully = stain

supercilious = arrogant

supplant = replace

surly = rude, crass

surmise = to guess

surmount = overcome

surreptitious = secretive

sustenance = supplying the necessities of life

swarthy = dark (as in complexion)

Sybarite = pleasure-seeker, lover of luxury

sycophant = flatterer, flunky

taciturn = who does not talk much

talon = claw of an animal

tantamount = equivalent

tawdry = gaudy, cheap

temerity = boldness

ample = enough, spacious, abundant

amplify = enlarge, increase, intensify

ancillary = supplementary, subsidiary, subordinate

anomaly = deviation from the rule, irregularity

artifact (BRITISH = artefact) = an object made by human, of historical interest

artisan = a skilled handicraftsman

authoritarian = dictator, extremely strict, bossy

autocrat = dictator or a high ranking government officer

bifurcated = divided into two branches, forked

blatant = glaring, obvious, showy

bountiful = abundant, plentiful

brazen = bold, shameless, impudent

breach = breaking of a rule, agreement, or law

caricature = cartoon, exaggerated portrait

carnivorous = meat-eating

catalyst = something that causes change without being changed

centripetal = tending toward the center

chaotic = in utter disorder

chauvinist = a man who thinks men are better than women

complement = To make complete, perfect

composure = Calmness of appearance

compress = to reduce, squeeze

constituent = electorate, component, part

constraint = something that limits what you can do

correlation = mutual relationship, association

corrugate = to wrinkle or draw into folds

depose = testify, to remove from a high position

depreciate = To lessen the worth of

determinate = Definitely limited or fixed, conclusive

dexterous = skillful, adroit

dwindle = To diminish or become less

earthy = crude

entity = being, existence

equity = impartiality, justice

equivocal = Ambiguous, open to two interpretations

eulogy = high praise

exotic = Foreign, romantic

extemporaneous = unrehearsed

fabricate = construct

fallible = Capable of erring

felicitous = very appropriate, pertinent

flair = a natural aptitude

flaunt = to show off

flora = plants

fraudulent = Counterfeit

fusion = union, coalition

germinate = To begin to develop into an embryo or higher form

heterogeneous = composed of unlike parts, different

hypothetical = theoretical, speculative

immune = Exempt, as from disease

imprudent = unwise

inception = The beginning

inconsequential = Valueless

indefatigable = never getting tired

indicative = suggestive, implying

indisputable = not disputed, unquestioned

infantile = childish, immature

ingenuous = naïve and unsophisticated

injurious = harmful

innovate = to invent, modernize

integrity = decency, honest, wholeness

intermittent = starting and stopping

introspective = looking within oneself

introvert = To turn within

invoke = request assistance or protection

iota = A small mark or part

irreverent = disrespectful

jaundice = disease of yellowish discoloration of skin

lackluster (BRITISH = lacklustre) = dull, dreary, colorless

laudable = Praiseworthy

lexicon = A dictionary

litigation = lawsuit

lunar = related to the moon

luscious = Rich, sweet, and delicious

metaphor = figure of speech comparing two different things

microcosm = The world on a small scale

migratory = Wandering from place to place with the seasons

mishap = Misfortune

mnemonic = related to memory

monotony = A lack of variation

omnivorous = eating everything

opportunist = One who takes advantage of circumstances

orifice = a small opening

overt = open to view

paradox = seemingly in contradiction

parasite = one who lives at another's expense

patent = the right to make or sell a new invention

pediatrician (BRITISH = paediatrician) = a child doctor

perusal = reading carefully

plenitude = Abundance

polyglot = Speaking several tongues

propagate = To spread

reactionary = related to, or favoring reaction

reciprocate = To give and take mutually

regimen = government rule, systematic plan

rehabilitate = To restore to a former status

reminiscence = remembrance of past events

renegade = rebel, dissident

resilient = the quality of springing back

retroactive = applying to an earlier time

sensual = related to the physical senses

strident = rough, harsh, caustic, loud

subliminal = subconscious, imperceptible

superannuated = retired

superficial = shallow and phony

supple = Easily bent

synchronous = happening at the same time

tainted = contaminated, corrupt

talisman = an object supposed to bring good luck

theocracy = government by the priests

therapeutic = medicinal

tortuous = with bends or turns

transcend = To surpass

transmute = To change in nature or form

tribute = a gift or statement showing respect

turbulence = violent agitation

unobtrusive = inconspicuous, not blatant

vent = small opening, outlet

verisimilitude = appearance of being true

versatile = adaptable, all-purpose

vicarious = substitute, surrogate

viscous = sticky, gluey, thick

warranty = guarantee of a product's soundness

wax = increase, grow

weather = endure the effects of weather or other forces

yoke = join together, unite

temporal = limited by time, secular, not lasting forever

tenacious = persistent

tendentious = biased

tenet = doctrine, principle

tensile = capable of being stretched

tenuous = thin, insubstantial

tepid = lukewarm

terse = concise, brief

tether = tie down, tie with a rope

thrall = slave

thwart = to block or prevent from happening

timorous = fearful, timid

tirade = scolding speech

toady = fawner, sycophant

torpid = lethargic, inactive

transient = fleeting, temporary

translucent = clear, lucid, almost transparent

travesty = caricature, farce, parody

trenchant = incisive, penetrating

trepidation = fear

trite = commonplace, insincere

truculent = fierce, savage, tending to argue a lot

truism = self-evident truth

tryst = meeting, rendezvous

tumult = commotion

turbid = muddy, clouded

turgid = Swollen, not flowing

turpitude = Depravity, evil

tyro = beginner

umbrage = resentment

unctuous = insincere

unkempt = messy in appearance

unsullied = spotless

usurp = seize, to appropriate

usury = overcharge, lending money at illegal rates of interest

vacillate = To waver

vacuous = inane, empty, not showing intelligence or purpose

vapid = vacuous, insipid

venal = willing to do wrong for money

vendetta = grudge, feud

venerable = respected because of age

verdant = green, lush

vex = annoy, to irritate

vicissitude = changing fortunes

vie = compete

vignette = scene, decorative design

vilify = defame

vindicate = free from blame

virile = manly

virulent = deadly, poisonous

vitiate = spoil, ruin

vitriolic = scathing, burning

vociferous = adamant, clamoring

volition = free will

voluminous = bulky, extensive, or great quantity

wallow = indulge, luxuriate

wan = sickly pale

wane = dissipate, wither

wary = guarded, careful

welter = confusion, hodgepodge

whet = stimulate, to sharpen

wily = shrewd, clever

winsome = charming

wizened = shriveled

wraith = ghost

wry = twisted, amusing

zephyr = gentle breeze, west wind

amphibian = creature that lives on land and water

anachronism = Anything occurring or existing out of its proper time

angular = Sharp-cornered or sharp angled

anthropomorphous = Nonhuman having or resembling human form or quality

apothegm = a short saying

appraise = assess, evaluate the value

arable = suitable for cultivation

asperity = roughness of temper

assay = to analyze or estimate

audit = formal examination of final records

augury = prophecy or prediction of events

aver = to declare to be true

aversion = intense dislike

aviary = cage where birds are kept

banter = to tease playfully and in good humor

beatific = supremely happy, angelic, saintly

benighted = un enlightened

benison = Blessing

blanch = bleach, whiten, to take the color out

bludgeon = to hit someone several times with a heavy object

bolster = To support or make something strong

burnish = To make brilliant or shining

canny = clever and able to think quickly, especially about money or business

carnal = of the flesh, sensual

carp = to find faults, complain constantly

cavalcade = a procession or sequence

celerity = quick moving or acting

cession = Surrender, as of possessions or rights

champ = to chew noisily

chastise = to criticize or punish someone

chattel = piece of personal property

churlish = rude, ungracious

circumscribe = To confine within bounds

clairvoyant = who can see the future, having ESP

collate = to sort or put in proper order

complaisant = Agreeable, friendly

consequential = important

contumacious = rebellious

cuisine = cookery, style of cooking

culmination = climax, final stage

curator = in charge of a library or museum

daunt = to frighten, subdue

declivity = a place that declines or slopes downwards

deranged = insane, delirious, maniacal

derivative = copied or adapted, not original

descry = To discern, to discover or reveal

diffidence = shyness, lack of confidence

dirge = lament with music, funeral hymn

discomfit = To put to confusion, discomfort

discordant = harsh-sounding, badly out of tune

dissimulate = to disguise

distaff = the female branch of a family

dolt = a stupid person

domineer = to rule over something in a tyrannical way

doughty = brave, dauntless

dross = waste matter, worthless impurities

dyspeptic = suffering from indigestion, gloomy and irritable

effluvium = noxious smells

effusive = expressing emotion without restraint

elation = exhilaration, joy

eloquence = fluent and effective speech

emollient = cream for softening, making supple

ensconce = to hide safely, settle comfortably

enunciate = verbalize, articulate

epilogue = The close of a narrative or poem

epitome = A simplified representation

equestrian = one who rides on horseback

excoriate = to denounce

exculpate = to clear of blame or fault

expatiate = to discuss in detail, elaborate

expatriate = who does not live in one's own country

expurgate = to purify by removing obscenities

extrinsic = not inherent or essential, coming from without

extrovert = an outgoing person

fell = to chop, cut down

fervid = fervent, passionate

fetter = to restrain, to bind

finicky = meticulous, fussy

fissure = a crack or break

flaccid = limp, flabby, weak

flamboyant = Characterized by extravagance

fluster = confuse

forbearance = Patient endurance or toleration of offenses

forte = A strong point

fractious = wayward, unruly, disorderly

frenzied = feverishly fast, hectic

funereal = mournful, appropriate to a funeral

gall = bitterness, nerve

gambol = Playful leaping or frisking

gaunt = thin, emaciated

gustatory = relevant to the sense of tasting

hallow = to make holy

hoary = white, old

holocaust = widespread destruction

ignominious = Shameful

impious = not devout in religion

implacable = unappeasable, merciless

improvident = lacking foresight or thrift

incarnadine = blood-red in color

indenture = bound to another by contract

interstice = a small space between things

iridescent = showing many colors

jettison = to throw overboard, abandon

jingoism = extremely aggressive and militant patriotism

lackadaisical = Listless, idle

languor = Lassitude of body or depression

lapidary = relating to precious stones

latitude = freedom from narrow limitations

lionize = treat as a celebrity

loiter = dawdle, loaf

lull = moment of calm

maritime = Situated on or near the sea

megalomania = mental state with delusions of wealth and power

mendacious = Untrue

meretricious = Alluring by false or gaudy show

molt = to shed hair, skin periodically

monastic = related to monks

morbid = abnormally gloomy

naiveté = a lack of worldly wisdom

nihilism = a belief in nothing, extreme skepticism

nomadic = moving from place to place

non sequitur = an irrelevant conclusion

nuptial = relating to marriage

objurgate = to chide, scold

opalescent = iridescent, displaying colors

ornithologist = scientist who studies birds

orotund = pompously said

palette = board for mixing paints

pastiche = imitation of another's style

patricide = murder of one's own father

peculation = theft of money or goods

pediment = triangular gable on a roof or façade

penumbra = partial shadow in an eclipse

permeable = penetrable

philology = study of words

plaintiff = injured person in a lawsuit

plangent = plaintive, resounding sadly

politic = expedient, prudent, well devised

potable = suitable for drinking

presentiment = sense of foreboding

primordial = existing at the beginning, rudimentary

pummel = beat, attack

putrid = dirty, rotten

quintessence = The most essential part of anything

ramshackle = dilapidated, falling to pieces

ratiocination = reasoning

raucous = Harsh sounding

ravenous = extremely hungry

rectitude = moral uprightness

refectory = dining hall

remediable = capable of being corrected

remonstrate = to protest or object

retinue = group of attendants

rococo = ornate, highly decorated

roil = to disturb or cause disorder

salubrious = healthy

serenity = calm, peacefulness

serrated = toothed, with a zigzag edge

sinuous = Curving in and out

slough = to discard or shed

sluggard = lazy, inactive person

sophist = person good at arguing deviously

sophomoric = immature and overconfident

staccato = marked by abrupt, clear-cut sounds

succinct = Concise

synthetic = artificial, imitation

threnody = a sad poem or song, dirge

tremulous = trembling, fearful

tundra = treeless plain found in Arctic or sub arctic regions

upbraid = to scold sharply

vagrant = An idle wanderer

variegated = many-colored

vaunted = boasted, bragged

veracious = truthful, accurate

verity = Truth

vernal = related to spring

wrangle = loud quarrel

abase = lower, humiliate

abash = humiliate, embarrass

abdicate = give up power or position

abeyance = postponement, temporary suspension

abhor = detest, loathe

abjure = renounce, to formally reject or abandon

ablution = cleansing, washing

abortive = unsuccessful, interruptive while incomplete

abrogate = cancel, to abolish by authority

absolve = acquit, to forgive or free from blame

abstruse = difficult to comprehend

abut = touch, border on

abysmal = deficient, sub par

accede = yield, express approval, agree to

acclimate = accustom oneself to a climate

acclivity = ascent, incline

accolade = applause, praise

accost = to approach and speak to someone

accouter (BRITISH = accoutre) = equip

acme = summit, highest point

acquiesce = to agree, comply passively

acrid = harsh, bitter, pungent, caustic

acrimonious = caustic, bitter

actuate = induce, start

acumen = sharpness of insight

adamant = insistent, uncompromising, unyielding

adduce = offer as example

adjunct = addition, something added, attached, or joined

admonish = warn gently, caution, or reprimand

adroit = skillful, accomplished, highly competent

adulation = applause, high praise

advent = arrival

adventitious = accidental

aegis = that which protects

affect = influence

affray = public brawl

agape = openmouthed, wonder

aggrandize = exaggerate, to make larger or greater in power

aghast = horrified

alacrity = swiftness, speed, cheerful willingness, eagerness

allay = to reassure; to lessen, ease, or soothe

allege = assert without proof

allegory = fable, symbolic representation

alliteration = repetition of the same sound

allude = refer to indirectly

amenable = agreeable

amiss = wrong, out of place

amity = Friendship

amorous = strongly attracted to love; showing love

amorphous = shapeless

amortize = to diminish by installment payments

amuck = murderous frenzy

anarchist = terrorist

animadversion = critical remark

animus = hate

annals = historical records

apocalyptic = ominous, doomed

apoplexy = stroke

appall (BRITISH = appal) = horrify

apparition = phantom

appellation = title, name

apposite = apt

apropos = Appropriate

arbiter = judge

archetype = original model

argot = slang

aria = operatic song

array = arrangement

arroyo = gully

artifice = trick

aseptic = sterile

atelier = workshop

avuncular = like an uncle

azure = sky blue

badger = To pester

badinage = banter, teasing conversation

bagatelle = nonentity, trifle

bandy = discuss lightly

bard = poet

baroque = ornate

bask = take pleasure in, sun

bauble = A trinket, trifle

beatitude = state of bliss

begrudge = resent, envy

beholden = in debt

bereft = deprived of

beset = harass, surround

besmirch = slander, sully

bicameral = having two legislative branches

bivouac = encampment

blase = bored with life

bode = portend

bogus = forged, false

brackish = salty

bucolic = rustic

burlesque = farce

cache = hiding place

cadaverous = haggard

callow = inexperienced

canine = pertaining to dogs

captious = fond of finding fault in others

carafe = bottle

cardinal = chief

carrion = decaying flesh

cascade = small waterfall

casuistry = clever argument to trick people

cauterize (BRITISH = cauterise) = to sear

chafe = abrade

chaste = pure, virgin

chasten = castigate

cipher = zero

cleft = split

clique = a small group

cloven = split

codicil = supplement to a will

cogitate = ponder

cognizant = aware

cohere = To stick together

cohort = an associate

comport = to conduct oneself

conch = spiral shell

concordat = Agreement

condescend = patronize, talk down to, to treat someone as though you are better

condiment = seasoning

condolence = sympathy for the family or friends of a person who has recently died

coniferous = bearing cones

consort = spouse

contagion = infectious agent

contingent = conditional

contort = twist

controvert = dispute

cordon = bond, chain

corollary = consequence

corpulent = fat

cortege = procession

coruscate = sparkle

covenant = agreement, pact

crestfallen = dejected

crevice = crack

cruet = small bottle

cull = pick out, select

culvert = drain

curry = seek favor by flattery

cynosure = celebrity

dank = damp

dauntless = courageous

deadpan = expressionless

debonair = sophisticated, affable

decant = pour

decrepitude = enfeeblement

defamation = slander

deflect = turn aside

defray = pay

deign = condescend

delirium = mental confusion, ecstasy

delve = dig, explore (of ideas)

demeanor (BRITISH = demeanour) = behavior

demented = deranged

demure = sedate, reserved

denizen = dweller

denouement = resolution

deposition = testimony

depredation = preying on, plunder

derelict = negligent

desolate = forsaken

desuetude = disuse

dialectic = pertaining to debate

diminution = Reduction

disconcert = confuse

discretion = prudence

dishevel = muss

disinter = unearth

disinterested = Impartial

disputatious = fond of arguing

disquisition = elaborate treatise

dissolute = profligate, immoral

dissonance = Discord

distrait = preoccupied, absent-minded

doggerel = poor verse

dolorous = gloomy

dregs = residue, riffraff

drone = speak in a monotonic voice

duenna = governess

ecclesiastical = churchly

eclat = brilliance

educe = draw forth, evoke

effete = worn out

effusion = pouring forth

elegiac = sad

emblazon = imprint, brand

embryonic = rudimentary

emeritus = retired, but retaining title

enamored (BRITISH = enamoured) = charmed, captivated

enclave = area enclosed within another region

engross = captivate

epoch = era

escapade = adventure

eviscerate = disembowel

ex officio = by virtue of position

excision = removal

exegesis = interpretation

exigency = urgency

exiguous = scanty

expletive = oath

extant = existing

extirpate = seek out and destroy

extrude = force out

facet = aspect

factious = causing disagreement

factitious = artificial

factotum = handyman

faux pas = false step, mistake

febrile = feverish, delirious

ferment = turmoil

ferret = rummage through

fervor (BRITISH = fervour) = intensity

fester = decay

festive = joyous

fete = to honor

fiat = decree

firebrand = agitator

flagellate = whip

flail = whip

foray = raid

fortitude = patience, courage

fret = worry

fritter = squander

frivolity = playfulness

fruition = realization, completion

galvanize = excite to action

gamut = range

garnish = decorate

genealogy = ancestry

genesis = beginning

genuflect = kneel in reverence

ghastly = horrible

glean = gather

gnome = dwarf-like being

gorge = stuff, satiate

gory = bloody

grapple = struggle

grisly = gruesome

guffaw = laughter

gusto = Keen enjoyment

guttural = throaty

haggard = gaunt

halcyon = serene

hale = healthy

hamper = obstruct

harbor (BRITISH = harbour) = give shelter, conceal

harridan = hag or an ugly old woman

harry = harass

heedless = careless

hegira = a journey to a more pleasant place

hibernal = wintry

histrionic = overly dramatic

homily = sermon

horde = group

hortatory = inspiring good deeds

hovel = shanty, cabin

hoyden = tomboy, boisterous girl

hubris = arrogance

hummock = knoll, mound

humus = soil

ichthyology = study of fish

idyllic = natural, picturesque

immolate = sacrifice

impale = pierce

impetus = stimulus, spark

impinge = encroach, touch

imponderable = difficult to estimate

imprimatur = sanction

impunity = exemption from harm

impute = charge

inalienable = that which cannot be taken away

incantation = chant

incapacitate = disable

inclement = harsh

incriminate = accuse

incubus = nightmare

ineffable = inexpressible

ineluctable = inescapable

infidel = nonbeliever

influx = inflow

infraction = violation

inimitable = peerless

iniquitous = unjust, wicked

inopportune = untimely

inordinate = excessive

insensate = without feeling

insouciant = nonchalant

insubordinate = disobedient

integument = a covering

inveigle = lure

irresolute = hesitant, uncertain

jejune = barren

jostle = push, brush against

ken = range of comprehension

knave = con man

knead = massage

lacerate = tear, cut

lackey = servant

laity = laymen

lambent = softly radiant

lave = wash

lax = loose, careless

lectern = reading desk

limn = portray, describe

litany = list

litotes = understatement for emphasis

lout = goon

lupine = wolf-like

luxuriant = lush

maim = injure

manacle = shackle

marauder = plunderer

masticate = chew

matriarch = matron

maul = rough up

mausoleum = tomb

mayhem = mutilation

medley = mixture

melee = riot

mellifluous = sweet sounding

menial = humble, degrading

mete = distribute

miasma = toxin

mien = appearance, demeanor

minion = subordinate

minutiae = trivia

mire = marsh

miscegenation = intermarriage between races

miscellany = mixture of items

modish = chic

molten = melted

monolithic = large and uniform

mortify = humiliate

mottled = spotted

mountebank = charlatan

muffle = stifle, quiet

mulct = defraud

muse = ponder

muster = to gather one's forces

noncommittal = neutral, circumspect

nonplus = bring to a halt by confusion

nubile = marriageable

nugatory = useless, worthless

oaf = awkward person

obelisk = tall column, monument

obituary = eulogy

oblation = offering, sacrifice

obliquity = perversity

odoriferous = pleasant odor

offal = inedible parts of a butchered animal

offertory = church collection

ogle = flirt

onus = burden

opprobrium = disgrace

opus = literary work of musical composition

orison = prayer

paleontologist (BRITISH = palaeontologist) = one who studies fossils

palpitate = beat, throb

pandemonium = din, commotion

pander = cater to people's baser instincts

pantomime = mime

papyrus = paper

paramour = lover

parapet = rampart, defense

paroxysm = outburst, convulsion

parsimonious = stingy

parvenu = newcomer, social climber

passe = outmoded

pastoral = rustic

peculate = embezzle, steal

pedantic = bookish

pell-mell = in a confused manner

penurious = stingy

peregrination = wandering

perforce = by necessity

perigee = point when moon is nearest to the earth

perjury = lying

peroration = conclusion of an oration

petrify = calcify, shock

petty = trivial

petulant = irritable, peevish

picaresque = roguish, adventurous

pied = mottled, brindled

piquant = tart-tasting, spicy

platonic = nonsexual

plebiscite = referendum

plumb = measure

polity = methods of government

poltroon = coward

portend = signify, augur

prate = babble

preamble = introduction

preternatural = abnormal

prim = formal, prudish

primogeniture = first-born child

primp = groom

proboscis = snout

prod = urge

profusion = overabundance

propellant = rocket fuel

prophylactic = preventive

propound = propose

proscenium = platform, rostrum

prosody = study of poetic structure

provender = dry food, fodder

proviso = stipulation

puissant = strong

purblind = obtuse, dim-sighted

purgatory = limbo, netherworld

purloin = To steal

purview = range, understanding

putative = reputed

quail = shrink, cower

quaint = old-fashioned

qualms = misgivings

quarry = prey, game

quay = wharf

queasy = squeamish

quip = joke

quirk = eccentricity

quizzical = odd

quorum = majority

rabid = mad, furious

raiment = clothing

rankle = cause bitterness, resentment

realm = kingdom, domain

reconnaissance = surveillance

recrimination = countercharge, retaliation

recumbent = reclining

redolent = fragrant

redoubtable = formidable, steadfast

redundant = repetitious

reek = smell

refraction = bending, deflection

regale = entertain

remiss = Negligent

remnant = residue, fragment

remorse = guilt

rend = to tear apart

render = deliver, provide

rendezvous = a meeting

rendition = version, interpretation

reparation = amends, atonement

repartee = witty conversation

repellent = causing aversion

repercussion = consequence

repine = fret

reprieve = temporary suspension

reprimand = rebuke

reprisal = retaliation

retaliate = revenge

retribution = reprisal

reverent = respectful

reverie = daydream

rigor = harshness

rime = white frost

risible = laughable

roseate = rosy, optimistic

roster = list of people

rout = vanquish

rubicund = ruddy, having healthy reddish color

ruffian = brutal person, bully

rummage = hunt

ruse = trick

sacerdotal = priestly

salutary = good, wholesome

sanctimonious = self-righteous

sang-froid = coolness under fire

sanguinary = gory, murderous

sapid = interesting

sarcophagus = stone coffin

sartorial = pertaining to clothes

sate = satisfy fully

saturnine = gloomy

satyr = demigod, goat-man

savoir-faire = tact, polish

savor (BRITISH = savour) = enjoy

scarify = criticize

scurry = move briskly

scuttle = to sink

sebaceous = like fat

seclusion = solitude

sedulous = diligent

seethe = fume, resent

semblance = likeness

senescence = old age

sepulcher (BRITISH = sepulchre) = tomb

sequacious = eager to follow, ductile

serried = saw-toothed

shibboleth = password

shoal = reef

shrew = virago

sidereal = pertaining to the stars

sinewy = fibrous, stringy

skinflint = miser

skittish = excitable

skullduggery (BRITISH = skulduggery) = trickery

slander = defame

sleight = dexterity

slither = slide

smattering = superficial knowledge

smirk = smug look

snivel = whine

solvent = financially sound

somatic = pertaining to the body

spasmodic = intermittent

spate = sudden outpouring

spectral = ghostly

splenetic = peevish

spry = nimble

spume = foam

stanza = division of a poem

stoke = prod, fuel

stratum = layer

stupor = lethargy

sub rosa = in secret

substantiate = verify

substantive = substantial

succor (BRITISH = succour) = help, comfort

succumb = yield, submit

suffuse = pervade, permeate

sultry = sweltering

sunder = split

sundry = various

supernumerary = subordinate

suture = surgical stitch

sylvan = rustic

tantalize = tease

taper = candle

tarn = small lake

tarry = linger

taurine = bull-like

taut = tight, stretched

temperate = moderate

tempo = speed

tentative = provisional

tenure = status given after a period of time

terrapin = turtle

testy = petulant

thespian = actor

throes = anguish

throng = crowd

timbre = tonal quality, resonance

Titanic = huge

tithe = donate one-tenth

titular = in name only, figurehead

tocsin = alarm bell, signal

touchstone = standard

traduce = slander

travail = work, drudgery

tribunal = court

troglodyte = cave dweller

truckle = yield

tutelage = guardianship

tyranny = oppression

unassuming = modest

uncouth = uncultured, crude

undulate = surge, fluctuate

uniformity = sameness

unsavory (BRITISH = unsavoury) = distasteful, offensive

unscathed = unhurt

unseemly = unbecoming, improper

untenable = cannot be achieved

ursine = bear-like

uxorious = a doting husband

vagary = whim

vainglorious = conceited

valor (BRITISH = valour) = bravery

vanguard = leading position

vassal = subject

vehement = adamant

veneer = false front, façade

venial = excusable

venturesome = bold, risky

viand = food

victuals = food

visage = facial expression

viscid = thick, gummy

vitreous = glassy

vituperative = abusive

votary = fan, aficionado

vouchsafe = confer, bestow

vulpine = fox-like

waggish = playful

wastrel = spendthrift

waylay = ambush

wean = remove from nursing, break a habit

wheedle = coax

whimsical = capricious

wince = cringe

winnow = separate

wither = shrivel

wont = custom

wrath = anger, fury

wreak = inflict

wrest = snatch

writhe = contort

yen = desire

yore = long ago

aberration = different from normal or usual

abettor = encourager

abnegation = repudiation, self-sacrifice

abominate = to hate

abrade = to rub off a surface

abstemious = Characterized by self denial or abstinence

accretion = grow in size or increase in amount

acerbity = bitterness of speech or temper

acetic = related to vinegar

acidulous = sour in taste or manner

acquiescence = Passive consent

acquittal = release from blame (as by a court)

actuarial = calculating

acuity = sharpness

addiction = compulsive, habitual need

addle = To make inefficient or unable to think

adjuration = solemn urging

adjure = to request solemnly

admonition = Genteelly point out mistake

agility = nimbleness

agitation = excitement, uneasiness

alimentary = supplying nourishment

allure = appeal, attract

allusion = indirect reference

alluvial = soil deposits left by rivers

amalgamate = To mix or join together to become one

amazon = female warrior

ambrosia = food of the Greek gods that provided immortal youth & beauty, anything sweet and pleasing

andirons = metal supports in a fireplace

anneal = to gradually heat and cool in order to soften, reduce brittleness

annuity = An annual payment or income

antecede = To precede

anthropoid = manlike

apiary = A place where bees are kept

apogee = The climax

apothecary = One who keeps drugs for sale and puts up prescriptions

appurtenances = subordinate possessions

aquiline = like an eagle, bent, booked, curved

arcade = a roofed passage between shops

archaeology = the study of ancient cultures by looking for and examining their buildings, tools

aromatic = fragrant

arrant = Notoriously bad

asceticism = doctrine of self-denial

assessment = estimation

astronomical = enormously large or extensive

athwart = across, opposition

aureole = sun's corona, halo

auroral = pertaining to the aurora borealis

auscultation = act of listening to the heart or lungs to discover abnormalities

austerity = quality of being self disciplined

baffle = to frustrate or unable to understand

bandanna = large, bright-colored handkerchief

barb = sharp projection from fishhook

barrage = a lot of questions or criticism

barter = to give in exchange rather than paying money

bassoon = reed instrument of the woodwind family

bate = let down, restrain

bawdy = indecent, obscene

bedizen = dress with vulgar finery

bedraggle = wet thoroughly

befuddle = confuse thoroughly

behoove = to be fit, to be right

benignant = Benevolent in feeling, character

bereavement = state of being deprived of something valuable or beloved

bete noire = aversion

betrothal = Engagement to marry

bibulous = Fond of drinking

bigotry = discrimination, prejudice

blasphemous = profane, impious

blazon = print or decorate something in a very noticeable way

blurt = to say something suddenly and without thinking, especially when you are excited or nervous

boorish = Rude

bouillon = clear beef soup

Bowdlerize = To expurgate in editing

braggadocio = someone who boasts

brazier = An open pan or basin for holding live coals

brindled = tawny or grayish with streaks or spots

brittle = Fragile

brocade = rich, gaudy fabric

brooch = a piece of jewelry for women which is fastened onto clothes with a pin

buffoonery = coarse jokes, etc

bugaboo = bugbear, object of baseless terror

bumptious = full of offensive self-conceit

bungle = to do something wrong in a very careless or stupid way

buskin = thick-soled half boot worn by actors of Greek tragedy

buxom = plump, vigorous, jolly

cameo = when someone famous appears for a short time in a film or play

canker = any ulcerous sore, any evil

canto = part of an extended poem

caparison = showy harnesser, ornamentation for a horse

caprice = A whim

carillon = a set of bells capable of being played

carmine = rich red

carousal = To drink deeply and in boisterous or jovial manner

carte blanche = complete freedom to do what you want

caryatid = sculptured column of a female figure

caste = one of the hereditary classes in Hindu society

catapult = slingshot

catechism = book for religious instruction

censor = to prohibit publication by law

centaur = mythical figure, half man and half horse

cerebration = thought

chaff = worthless products of an endeavor

chasm = a long, deep, narrow hole in rock or ice

chiropodist = one who treats disorders of the feet

chivalrous = courteous to ladies

ciliated = having minute hairs, one-celled animal

circlet = small ring, band

clangor (BRITISH = clangour) = loud, resounding noise

clarion = shrill, trumpet like sound

clavicle = collarbone

climactic = relating to the highest point

clime = region, climate

coadjutor = assistant, colleague

cockade = decoration worn on hat

coeval = living at the same time as contemporary

cog = a spoke in a wheel, a small and unimportant person

cohesion = consistency

colander = utensil with perforated bottom used for straining

collage = a picture made by sticking small pieces of paper or other materials

collier = worker in coal mine, ship carrying coal

colossal = huge

comely = a woman who is attractive in appearance

comestible = something fit to be eaten

comeuppance = rebuke, one's deserved fate or punishment

comity = courteousness, civility

conclave = private meeting

condign = adequate, deservedly severe

connivance = pretence of ignorance of something wrong, assistance or permission to offend

connubial = related to marriage or matrimony

cormorant = greedy, rapacious bird

cornice = a decorative border around the walls of a room close to the ceiling

corsair = pirate ship

covetous = very desirous of something, avaricious, greedy

coy = shy, modest

cozen = cheat, hoodwink, swindle

crabbed = sour, peevish

credo = a set of beliefs

crepuscular = pertaining to twilight

crone = hag

crotchet = a fancy, a whim, an eccentricity

cul-de-sac = a blind alley, a trap

dappled = spotted

dastard = A base coward

daub = to paint carelessly, to smear

dawdle = to waste time by trifling, to move slowly

debenture = bond issued to secure a loan

decollete = having a low-necked dress

decrepit = Enfeebled, as by old age or some chronic infirmity

deducible = derived by reasoning

defalcate = to misuse money put in trust

defection = desertion

deify = To regard as a god

deliquescent = capable of absorbing moisture from air and becoming liquid

delusion = Mistaken conviction

delusive = deceptive, raising vain hopes

demesne = domain

demolition = destruction

demoniacal = related to evil spirits, devilish

denotation = the exact literary meaning of a word, designation, definition

depilate = remove hair

derision = Ridicule

dermatologist = one who studies the skin and its diseases

descant = discuss fully

desideratum = that which is desired

despoil = to bereave, rob, plunder, strip of possessions

despotism = Any severe and strict rule

detergent = cleansing agent

detonation = explosion

devolve = to roll down, to hand down

diadem = crown

dint = means, effort

dipsomaniac = a person having an uncontrollable desire for alcohol, inebriate

disapprobation = rejection, disapproval

disavowal = Denial

dishabille = in a state of undress

dishearten = discourage, lose spirit

dismember = cut into small parts

disport = amuse

dissuasion = advise against

divergent = Tending in different directions

divination = The forecast of future events or discovery of what is lost or hidden

docket = a list of cases to be dealt with

doddering = shaky, infirm from old age

doff = take off

dorsal = belonging to the back side, posterior, tail

douse = to plunge into water, to extinguish

dowdy = slovenly, untidy

drudgery = Hard and constant work in any dull occupation

durance = confinement

eclipse = The obstruction of Sun by moon, or of moon by earth

eerie = weird

efflorescent = opening in flower

elusory = tending to deceive expectations

elysian = relating to paradise, blissful

emanate = to express a feeling or quality through the way one looks

emendation = corrections of errors

emetic = a medicine that causes vomiting

emolument = salary or fees for a job, remuneration, pay scale

empyreal = celestial, fiery

encomiastic = praising, eulogistic

Special Free Gift for You

GRE Vocab CD#1 Download

www.FranklinVocab.com/free.php

Support Email: sale@FranklinVocab.com

Special Thanks to These Students
for Helping Make This Book Better

GyuHyeon Choi

(Note: if you find any way to make this book more helpful to students,
please tell me and if I use it, your name will also appear here.)

Made in the USA
Middletown, DE
26 June 2017